Thinking Critically about New Age Ideas

❏ ❏ ❏ ❏ ❏ ❏ ❏

WILLIAM D. GRAY
Southwestern College

Wadsworth Publishing Company
Belmont, California
A Division of Wadsworth, Inc.

Philosophy Editor: Kenneth King
Editorial Assistant: Karen Jones
Production Editor: Jerilyn Emori
Designer: Kaelin Chappell
Print Buyer: Randy Hurst
Permissions Editor: Jeanne Bosschart
Copy Editor: William Waller
Compositor: G&S Typesetters, Inc.
Cover: Nancy Brescia

Printed in the United States of America   49

1 2 3 4 5 6 7 8 9 10—95 94 93 92 91

Library of Congress Cataloging-in-Publication Data

Gray, William D. (William Douglas)
   Thinking critically about New Age ideas / William D. Gray.
     p.   cm.
   Includes bibliographical references and index.
   ISBN 0-534-14394-6
   1. Occultism—Controversial literature.   2. Psychical
research—Controversial literature.   3. New Age
movement—Controversial literature.   4. Critical
thinking.   I. Title.
BF1042.G76   1990   90-37935
133—dc20   CIP

**This book is dedicated to
my mother and father**

CONTENTS

❏ ❏ ❏ ❏ ❏ ❏ ❏

PREFACE

❏   ❏   ❏   ❏   ❏   ❏   ❏

In recent years there has been a sharp increase of interest in phenomena that have not been given validation within the mainstream of science. So strong and pervasive is this fascination that it has acquired the identity of an actual movement: the New Age. The beliefs of this movement encompass every aspect of the paranormal, including channeling, clairvoyance, precognition, telepathy, psychic surgery, psychic healing, healing crystals, psychokinesis, astral travel, levitation, the Bermuda Triangle mystery, unidentified flying objects (UFOs), plant consciousness, auras, and ghosts. The movement also has revived many ancient occult beliefs—demonic possession, reincarnation, astrology, palmistry, and fortune telling—and it includes numerous psychological techniques for heightened awareness. Its central philosophy is that we create our own reality.

❏ Motivation

As an instructor of philosophy I became interested in paranormal topics because many of my students were bringing them up in class: "Is the Bermuda Triangle a time-warp?" "Hasn't channeling been proved?" "Isn't the police department making use of psychics to help solve crimes?" "Hasn't the truth about UFOs been covered up by the government?" "What about Uri Geller, the man who bends metal spoons with his mind?" These were ideas that my students obviously believed, and they never failed to provoke excited dialogue in the classroom.

After doing considerable research, I learned that serious scientific investigation had been done on practically all paranormal claims and had failed to validate any of them. It seemed astonishing to me that there could be such a great discrepancy between hard science and popular belief. Many people believe not only that there is overwhelming documentation of paranormal phenomena but also that they have proof of them from their own experience. Haven't we all, for example, experienced knowing who the caller is before we answer the phone (clairvoyance)? Or haven't we all known about an event before it happened (precognition)? Thus, many people can't help but wonder: why don't scientists recognize psychic phenomena and other aspects of the paranormal as real things?

It was this question that motivated me to design a course and write a book focusing on the paranormal. It was a natural: the topics are intrinsically interesting, and the students are already involved. The stage is perfect for teaching important critical-thinking skills. The course and this book are essentially an open-minded journey through the land of the paranormal seeking to understand why most scientists don't accept paranormal claims. I ask: what is it about the evidence for paranormal ideas and the popular reasoning used to support them that most scientists find wanting?

❑ Objectives

One important goal of this book is to teach an understanding of the way in which scientists think when they are doing good science. In this way students learn the general method of science and also how to distinguish real science from pseudoscience. I've taken pains to represent science as an extremely practical method of "go and see" used by everybody when certainty is important, not as an arcane procedure restricted to the laboratory for a supereducated elite. The point is not to turn all students into science majors but to enable them to be more rigorous in their reasoning about paranormal topics and about matters of fact in daily life.

Another important goal is to build a sensitivity to the words and sentences we use to express paranormal ideas. The topic of the paranormal excites the imagination and the intellect and, by its very nature, invites speculative talk about intriguing possibilities. We easily soar beyond the familiar and the well-understood to delve into a world of mystery. This, I believe, is good: it is a liberating exercise for our minds. But as we do this, we run the risk of articulating ideas that are at best unclear and at worst nonsensical. To ensure that we are speaking coherently, we need to be aware of and stay in touch with linguistic requirements. Thus, the book begins (in Chapters 1 and 2) with a discussion of language. The main objective of these two chapters is to show when it's appropriate to look for evidence and when it isn't. In other words, the point is to be able to distinguish a paranormal possibility that might someday get scientific validation from one that could never do so.

A third goal of the book is to teach readers to identify an argument and to recognize classic cases of bad arguments as they occur in reasoning about the paranormal. Accordingly, Chapter 3, "Common Fallacies," presents 16 of the traditional informal fallacies found in many logic and critical-thinking texts, but it discusses them in connection with New Age ideas so that they can be recognized in that context.

Chapter 4, "The Paranormal," underlines the importance of the open mind and seeks to understand science's rejection of the paranormal by showing how open-mindedness and critical thinking work together in the search for truth. Factors that account for the widespread belief in the paranormal are explored and analyzed. In this chapter I also attempt to provide a balance to the New Age movement in three ways. The first is to encourage the search for commonsense explanations. The second way is to review the scientific facts that show some paranormal phenomena to be quite normal. The third way is to inform readers of literature reporting scientific investigations of paranormal claims.

The last chapter, "Science versus Pseudoscience," is designed to help students spot pseudoscience when it occurs. Twelve important characteristics of good science are listed and contrasted with those of pseudoscience. These signposts are illustrated through a continued discussion of New Age phenomena.

❑ Approach

Throughout the text I have endeavored to address issues that students find interesting, discuss them in terms that they can relate to, and write in a style that they find agreeable. Accordingly, the main text and the exercises attempt to meet the students on their own ground and teach critical-reasoning skills that they will find useful. Many of the examples were actually taken, sometimes verbatim, from discussions with people in and out of the classroom. Others were taken from my own personal investigations of phenomena reputed to be paranormal.

❏ Uses

I have written this book to be used in a logic or critical-thinking course, but it clearly has much wider applicability. Because the text is nontechnical throughout and presupposes no special background of any kind, it could easily be used as a supplement to enrich a wide variety of courses where critical reasoning, especially about the paranormal, is important.

Though it would be helpful to read the chapters in order, it is not strictly necessary to do so. Each chapter is sufficiently independent to allow a random approach if that is desired.

❏ Acknowledgments

I wish to thank Ken King, philosophy editor at Wadsworth, for being so supportive throughout the entire project. Special thanks, also, to Jerilyn Emori, production editor, who was most helpful and patient, and to Bill Waller, copy editor, who made the manuscript considerably more readable. A large number of improvements can be attributed to free-lance copy editor Ann Marie Dobbs, who was kind enough to read the original manuscript. The text has also benefited greatly from suggestions made by the following reviewers: Jeffrey Berger, Community College of Philadelphia; Robert M. Johnson, Castelton State College; David W. Paulsen, Evergreen State College; and Leslie C. Read, Sacramento City College. I owe a debt to John Wilson, author of *Language and the Pursuit of Truth,* and to Paul Kurtz, founder of the Committee for the Scientific Investigation of Claims of the Paranormal, whose writings have inspired and enlightened me in uncounted ways. Finally, I wish to thank my students whose numerous comments have been the guiding light from beginning to end.

CHAPTER I

❑ ❑ ❑ ❑ ❑ ❑ ❑

Language:
The Starting Point

It is indeed not the least of the logician's tasks to indicate the pitfalls laid by language in the way of the thinker.

Gottlob Frege

Critical thinking is the reasoning we do in order to determine whether a claim is true. This is a process we can do poorly or splendidly. Because our conclusions are only as sound as our reasoning processes, critical thinking is not a luxury but a necessity if we are serious about discovering the truth. The clear advantage to studying critical thinking, then, is that we become better able to sort out fact from fiction.

Thinking critically means proceeding patiently and cautiously, always checking for possible errors before we become confident that we know the truth. This is especially important when reasoning about New Age or paranormal ideas such as ESP, channeling, or precognition, because these topics remain under a heavy cloud of scientific controversy. A man may believe that he has ESP because he seems to know that his mother is calling even before he picks up the phone. Of course, he may actually have ESP, but before that conclusion can confidently be reached, a number of questions will occur to the critical thinker: How often do I "know" it's my mother and then discover that I'm wrong? Could my sometimes being right be a coincidence? Does my mother call at certain predictable times? Is my intuition real, or does it just seem real? How could it be tested to prove that it is real? These issues must all be addressed before we can know that ESP is really taking place. Until they are, the idea of ESP remains merely an interesting possibility.

To think critically about paranormal ideas, then, is to do our very best to find possible errors in our reasoning and to clarify the require-

1

ments of good reasoning. This task, generally speaking, is the aim of this book: it attempts to alert you to a broad spectrum of intellectual pitfalls that stand in the way of your quest for the truth about paranormal ideas.

We begin with language, because it is of fundamental importance in every act of reasoning. Some topics popular in New Age circles are intellectual dead ends that can be avoided only by developing an awareness of the nature and function of language. Lack of such awareness leads to a form of superstitious thinking in which words are regarded as magical entities possessing hidden meanings. When this superstition takes hold, we become absorbed in metaphysical speculation about mysterious entities, or we become involved in disputes that appear to be about fact but that are really about words.

❏ The Importance of Language Awareness

Because language is the medium by which we usually express our thoughts and ideas, it is perhaps the best place to start our exploration of thinking critically. At first glance it might seem that giving language our attention is a waste of time. After all, don't we already have mastery of our native tongue? And don't we communicate effectively a great majority of the time?

Of course, we do have mastery of our native language, and normally, communicating our intended message is no problem. But we don't always say what we think we're saying, and it's not always true that we're saying something sensible just because we think we are. The linguistic pitfalls that await us when we are speaking and writing can be extremely subtle, and to become conscious of them often requires extra effort of a special sort. It involves making a shift from our normal mode of thinking about people, things, events, and ideas to thinking about the words that we use to talk about them. This change requires some getting used to, but the effort we make should be repaid in a greatly improved capacity to think clearly and coherently.

Son: How high is up?

Mother: Your question makes no sense, because you're not using those words correctly.

Son: I don't care about words. I just want to know how high is up.

In this dialogue we can see that no progress will be made until the mother can direct her son's attention to the language he is using to ask his question. The child is not aware that he has broken the rules of English grammar, which say that he can ask "How high is the Empire State Building?" but not "How high is up?" The boy may feel certain that he has a legitimate question and become frustrated because his mother is dodging the issue. But once he sees that his question involves a linguistic error, he will know better than to continue to seek an answer to it.

Language and the Paranormal

The importance of language awareness increases proportionately as our thinking becomes more speculative. The more unusual an idea is, the more we feel language to be a limiting factor, and the less we are daunted by strange-sounding phrases. There may be justification for this feeling, but at the same time it cannot be denied that it is very easy to create terms and sentences that have a questionable meaning or no meaning at all. This issue becomes acutely important when we delve into New Age philosophy, because many of its ideas are bizarre as well as appealing and fascinating—a captivating combination. Thus, our objective in turning the spotlight on language will be to learn to avoid being duped by our own linguistic creations when we are thinking and speaking about paranormal subjects.

What Is Human Language?

A good way to start becoming aware of language is to clarify what human language is and how it works, because many problems arise from a misunderstanding of this basic issue. The term *language* covers many different things. We speak of body language, music as a universal language, the language of the bees, and so on. But when we speak of English or Chinese or Afrikaans as a language, we are talking about a system of communication that uses rule-governed symbols in the form of words and sentences. Animals, insects, and even plants communicate with one another, but they don't have language in this sophisticated sense of the term.

Animal Language Serious attempts have been made to teach sign language to apes so that they can make words and sentences. Washoe, a chimpanzee, and Koko, a gorilla, were apparently able to learn and use many signs to make sentences. Scientific critics have pointed out, however, that these animals do not combine these signs in a way that demonstrates an understanding of grammar and syntax, essential parts of human language. Moreover, these animals do not teach signing to their young, do not sign to each other conversationally, and sign only in close connection with a reward or a cue from their trainer. Such signing, the critics say, is not really signing (or symbolizing) at all but mere imitating and is entirely explainable in terms of operant conditioning (producing behavior patterns by rewards and punishments) (Terrace, 1979, cited in Goleman, 1982). In other words, the animals are simply learning new ways of getting food.

Evidently, human language is a complex system of communication not shared by any other creatures that we know. Another reason for believing this to be the case is that humans possess sites in the left hemisphere of the brain (Broca's area and Weineke's area) that are devoted to the production and processing of linguistic symbols. These sites are not found in apes, porpoises, or any other animals.

The Origin of Human Language   No one really knows exactly how our language got started, but scientific evidence makes two things very clear: in the early stages of human development we did not have language, and language developed over vast stretches of time as a result of our gradually evolving brain. These are two vitally important facts to remember if we are to avoid magical or superstitious thinking about language. From these facts we can derive four basic principles that will help us avoid magical or superstitious thinking about our language. They, in turn, will help us keep our feet on the ground, as it were, when discussing paranormal ideas.

Four Basic Principles of Human Language

Because the advent of language had to await the development of the human brain, the structure and content of existing language must be the result of human behavior and biology. Thus, our first basic principle is: *language is a human product*. We must not think that words and sentences somehow existed before humans evolved. Rather, we should think of humans coming on the scene first and then, later, words and sentences being created as useful tools of communication. If language is a human product, when a question arises regarding any aspect of language (for example, the meaning of a word or phrase or the proper use of a punctuation mark) the only authorities we can turn to are human beings, past or present.

Our second principle is a consequence of the first: *whatever meaning a word has is due to the use that humans put it to*. In other words, if we applied the word *tree* to certain four-legged animals instead of to those tall things that grow out of the ground, the meaning of *tree* would be different from what it now is.

The third principle can be derived from the second: *the meaning of a word is arbitrary*. It is really just an accident of history that we use the word *tree* to refer to trees and not to cows or stones. The connection between a particular object and our word for it was not preestablished.

The last principle seems like common sense, and it can also be derived from our three previous ones: *in order for there to be symbolic communication between people, there must be agreement on the use of those symbols*. In other words, you understand what I mean when I say "tree" because you and I apply this word in the same way. If I used the word *tree* to apply to four-legged creatures and you used it to apply to certain forms of vegetation, there would be a communication breakdown. Natural human languages are essentially complex systems of rules that are shared by vast numbers of people who can communicate with one another because they use words in the same way. This common, or ordinary, use is the source from which the vast majority of words get their meaning.

Meaning Variations

Because a word gets its meaning from the way it is used, the meaning of a word changes as the use changes; a word can take on new meanings or lose old ones as time and place vary. In the United States the word *gay*, for example, used to mean "merry," but today it is primarily used to mean "homosexual." In England a visitor from the United States might be puzzled if the host asked, "Would you like to douche?" In England that means to shower, but in the United States it means to bathe the female genitalia.

Or consider the word *conversation*. Between the years 1300 and 1740 (roughly) one of its meanings was the act of living among persons. Between 1594 and 1809 it acquired the meaning of sexual intercourse, and between 1620 and 1720 it came to mean being involved with something in business or study (for example, "John is having a conversation with his encyclopedia"). Today, this word has a quite different meaning (a verbal interchange of ideas between people), and it seems to have shed most of its old meanings.

So which one is the true meaning? This question is a bad one, because it shows ignorance of the fact that words are human-made symbols with constantly changing uses (meanings). Words are merely tools that humans use to do different jobs at different times and places.

❏ Linguistic Superstition

Historically, language has often been regarded with superstition. In some primitive tribes, for example, a warrior was not supposed to let enemy warriors know his name, because that would give them the power to kill him. In the Middle Ages knowing the proper names of devils and witches made it possible to invoke supernatural powers. In most ancient religions it was believed that many ailments could be cured by the mere repetition of healing words.

Today we have largely outgrown this attitude toward language, but we nevertheless do have our own form of linguistic superstition; it is just much subtler. As a general definition, let's say that *linguistic superstition* occurs *when we treat words as if they had a power of their own independent of human agency.* The medieval sorcerer who chanted a special word in order to tap an occult power believed that this word, and this word only, had a magical power to engage a mysterious force. The word was regarded not just as a tool created by humans for the purpose of communication but as an active agent itself.

A sophisticated form of linguistic superstition occurs when we puzzle over the ultimate meaning of a word independently of how human beings use it. Many perplexing philosophical questions reflect this attitude. Here are some examples:

What is truth?

What is time?

What is the mind?

What is the good?

What is knowledge?

What is reality?

These questions are not new. They come down to us from the early dawn of our intellectual history, and they are still the focus of great controversy and wonder. It sometimes seems that when we try to answer them, we get confused and lost. We want to throw up our hands and say: "No one really knows what truth is." "No one really knows what the mind is." "The mind is a mysterious thing."

But at the moment we become hooked on a mystery of this kind, we are engaged in a subtle form of linguistic superstition. We are regarding the word *truth,* for instance, as having a hidden meaning not known to human beings. That is, we are treating this word as if it could signify (mean something) without the help of human agents. We are, in other words, violating basic principles 1 and 2, which tell us that any word can have only the meaning that human beings give it. If we argue over the question of truth, it means that we are using the word *truth* in conflicting ways; it does not mean that we are ignorant of the real nature of truth.

Pseudomysteries

When we are captivated by mystery through linguistic superstition, it often feels as if we are trying to make out the details of a mysterious object of some kind. Take *time*, for example. We cannot see it, feel it, smell it, touch it, or taste it. It has no shape or color. So what is it? It is impossible to define without employing the word in its own definition. If we say that time is "a measurable duration" (as my *Webster's New Collegiate Dictionary* does), we have the problem of circularity, since the word *duration* cannot be defined without the word *time*. Perhaps we are not smart enough to know what time is. Perhaps time doesn't really exist and is just an illusion. No matter how you look at it, it seems that time is something mysterious.

But wait. Don't we set our alarm clocks to get up in the morning, and don't we use the word *time* frequently to communicate a clear message to other people? We say:

Take your time.

At what time does the class break?

He did not arrive in time for dinner.

The Korean War and the Vietnam War happened at different times.

After the speeches there will be no time for questions and
answers.

Our house has been broken into many times.

I lose my temper from time to time.

Clearly, we communicate beautifully with the word *time*. This shows
that we know what the word means. It also shows that *we know what
time is*. This is not surprising, because we invented the word. Time is a
mystery only when we look for something more to the word than we
put into it.

Let's take another example: the mind. The feeling of mystery about
the mind is expressed in various ways:

No one really knows what the mind is.

The mind is an intangible substance having no weight and oc-
cupying no space.

No one really knows the limits of the mind (and so we can't dismiss the possibility of ESP, astral travel, and channeling).

But again, the word *mind* is used constantly by all of us to communicate successfully. Here are some examples:

Make up your mind.

Einstein had a great mind.

Mind what you're doing.

Add 37 and 65 in your mind.

The national debt is so large it boggles the mind.

In Ralph's mind all women are no good.

Can it be true that we do not know what the mind really is or what the
word *mind* really means? Can it be true that we don't actually know
what we're talking about whenever we use this word? No, because the
word functions perfectly to communicate clear information in our
daily lives. The mystery arises only if we are looking for a thing or an
entity called the mind, and this search springs from the superstitious
idea that the mind has more meaning than we give it.

Of course, the phony mystery of the mind should not be confused
with the legitimate questions of science about how the brain functions.
What happens in the brain, for example, when we dream, calculate, ex-

perience terror, or get hungry? These are questions that scientific research seeks to answer, and they indicate that we still have much to learn about the brain.

There is also much we can learn about the mind. For example, does learning while we are asleep really work? Can we learn to control our dreams in a way that would be therapeutic? Can memory be improved? Can we move objects by just thinking about them? Or can we read the thoughts of another person? These are legitimate questions that scientific research can answer.

When I say that the mystery of the mind is a pseudomystery, I don't mean to suggest that we don't have a mind. Of course we do. That is, we think, remember, calculate, and dream. But to say that we do these things is not to say that we are in possession of a mysterious thing with mysterious powers.

Real Mysteries

Of course, not all mysteries are spurious. Take quasars, for example. Quasars are the most distant objects known to us and can be seen only with very powerful radio telescopes. (*Quasar* stands for quasi-stellar radio source.) They are from 10 billion to 15 billion light-years away. They are a mystery to us because we do not know how to explain such rapid fluctuations of such enormous quantities of energy.

What makes quasars a genuine mystery and not a phony one? It is the fact that this mystery springs from observations and not just from words. When we puzzle over quasars, we are scratching our heads trying to figure out how to explain what we see. But when we puzzle over the nature of time or the mind, it is not the oddness of something observed that intrigues us. Indeed, part of the mystery stems from the fact that time or the mind are *not* observable things. We have a word (*time* or *mind*) that we feel must stand for something, but something illusive. The word seems like an arrow pointing to a hidden object.

Thus, the genuine mystery is created by strange facts observed, whereas the pseudomystery is a feeling of puzzlement (produced by linguistic superstition) over the illusive referent (or meaning) of a word.

❏ Verbal Disputes

We can also find a subtle form of linguistic superstition in what are called verbal disputes. A verbal dispute occurs when two or more people think that they are arguing about objects named by their words when, in fact, they are really arguing about the words themselves. The reason that such disputes are lengthy and often unresolved is that the disputants don't realize that they are *merely arguing over words*. For example, imagine the following account, and then listen to the dispute that ensues:

> A hunter is trying to shoot a squirrel perched on the trunk of a tree. As the hunter approaches and takes aim, the squirrel moves to the other side of the trunk, where the hunter cannot see it. The hunter begins moving around the tree to catch sight of the squirrel. As he does this, the clever squirrel moves around the trunk of the tree and always manages to keep the tree between itself and the hunter. The hunter makes a complete circle around the tree, but the squirrel has stayed out of sight the whole time. The question is, did the hunter go around the squirrel?
>
> *Joe:* The squirrel never let the hunter go around it, because it kept its belly to him the whole time. Thus, the hunter did not go around the squirrel.
>
> *Jim:* I disagree. The hunter *did* go around the squirrel, because he made a complete circle, and the squirrel was inside it.
>
> *Joe:* That's ridiculous. The hunter did not go around the squirrel, because he was always facing the squirrel's belly. In order to go around the squirrel, he would have to be first facing its belly, then facing its left side, then facing its back, then facing the other side, then facing its belly again.
>
> *Jim:* It doesn't matter what the squirrel was doing as long as it was inside the circle made by the hunter. The hunter had to go around the squirrel, because he made a complete circle with the squirrel inside.

Joe and Jim are involved in a dispute that could be lengthy and exasperating. Controversies of this kind frequently go nowhere and create needless friction between people.

Facts Don't Help

What makes this dispute so frustrating is that there are no experts, no reference books, and no factual data anywhere that could settle it. It is the nature of this type of dispute that it *cannot be resolved by an inves-*

tigation into the facts. There are no scholars or scientists who could provide the answer to this question. No matter what "authorities" you choose to put this question to, some of them would say yes, some of them would say no, and (if they're sensitive to the pitfalls of language) some would say that it all depends on your definition of *go around*.

Factual disputes are *about facts,* not words, and they are *settled only by getting more factual information.* Here's an example:

Dave: Lincoln was born in Indiana. I learned that in third grade.

Marv: No, he wasn't. He was born in Kentucky. It says so in my college textbook.

Dave and Marv can continue to argue about this, but there is no point in doing so, because there are facts that can settle it. Careful and thorough research into the facts will uncover information showing that one of them is right (Marv) and the other one is wrong. It is the mark of a *factual dispute* that *a resolution can be obtained only through the gathering of more factual information.*

Settling a Verbal Dispute

When uncovering more facts cannot provide an answer to our question, it is not a factual question but a verbal one. "Does the hunter go around the squirrel?" is not a question about facts; it is *a question about how we should use words.* The only way to deal with it is to say that it all depends on what you mean by *go around.* The only possible resolution to a controversy of this kind is for the disputants to converge on a particular way of speaking or to simply recognize and respect each other's verbal preference.

A Linguistic Illusion

Why do Joe and Jim get so worked up about this issue if it's merely about words? The reason, it seems, is that they *think they are arguing about facts.* If they fully realized that the difference between them is merely one of verbal preference, there would be little or no cause for anger. They are deceived by the question "Did the hunter go around the squirrel?" because it looks like a factual question, such as "Did the hunter shoot the squirrel?"

But why should they think that they're arguing about facts? The answer seems to be that they are both regarding the term *go around* as if it had a significance before human beings entered the picture. They forget (if they ever knew) that the term means only whatever we use it to mean. This is a linguistic superstition that violates basic principle 1: language is a human product.

Criteria

Let's look more closely at what is going on in the argument between Joe and Jim. Joe is using the words *go around* to mean first facing the front, then facing the side, then the back, then the front again of an object. This is his criterion for applying the word. Jim, on the other hand, has a different criterion. The squirrel needs only to be inside the hunter's completed circle for him to use *go around*.

Because Joe and Jim use the same words in different ways (different criteria), the same words have two different meanings here. No wonder that their dispute cannot be resolved; they are not even speaking the same language! It would have been better if they had used different words altogether. The fact that they use the same words makes it look as if they are talking about the same thing. But they aren't. In order for the same word to have the same meaning, the same criteria must be employed. *If the criteria are different, the meanings are different.* The futility of continuing an argument is obvious when we see that different meanings are attached to the same word.

A Serious Issue: Abortion

The fact that people do get worked up is the whole point in dealing with verbal issues in a book on critical thinking. People are injured, wars are fought, and thousands die over issues that are merely verbal. Let's take a current example that's fairly hot: is the four-week-old human embryo a human being or not?

> *Sue:* The four-week-old embryo is not a human being, because it cannot live outside the mother's body and independently of her support, as a baby can. A baby is a human being, but a four-week-old embryo is not.

> *Val:* Ridiculous! The need for a life-support system has nothing to do with it. Is an adult who must be connected to a heart machine any less human? The four-week-old embryo is just a very young human being. At this stage the brain and nervous system are start-

ing to form. In fact, it has everything it needs, given enough time, to develop into a normal adult.

This dispute is quite serious, because it bears directly on the issue of abortion. If the four-week-old embryo is a human being, abortion at this stage could be called murder. If it isn't, abortion could not constitute murder. Emotions run high, and people even come to blows over this question.

That people argue intensely about this issue shows that they do not regard it as merely a verbal question. This question, they feel, is about a fact, not about a word. They feel that it's a question about the true nature of the object that the term *human being* names, not a question about how we do or should use this term (a common symptom of verbal superstition). In his first term in office President Ronald Reagan formed a committee of assorted scholars, scientists, and theologians to answer this question. It is very unlikely that he would have devoted so much time, money, and attention to this question if he had regarded it as merely verbal.

But that's all it is! In spite of our vast store of accumulated knowledge about the embryo in the fourth week, we know of no facts that answer this question for everyone. And we know of no possibilities that, should they be later discovered as facts, would make everyone agree that the question had been answered. When medical scientists are asked this question, some say yes, some say no, and some dismiss it by saying that it isn't a scientific question. If it were a scientific question, it could be answered by discovering new facts. But any new facts, when they are discovered, do not settle the issue. People are divided over how to interpret those facts, and the controversy continues. Thus, we can see that what seems like a question about fact is really just a question about how we should use a certain word.

Inventing New Meanings

Verbal disputes arise because people differ (for whatever reason) in their use of the same word. In two disputes discussed previously (involving *go around* and *human being*) the disputants both used the same term within the rules of ordinary usage. In other words, there was nothing unusual about their uses of the term. People sometimes do use *go around* as Joe did, and they sometimes use it the way Jim did. The criteria each of them used are actually employed in everyday English.

The same could be said of *human being*. People sometimes use the criteria Sue used, and they sometimes use the criteria Val used.

But it sometimes happens that one of the disputants uses a term according to criteria that practically nobody ever uses. In this case the verbal disagreement can produce an even deeper level of confusion. For example, consider the following dispute:

> *Rick:* The Holocaust [the systematic extermination of the Jews during the second world war] was the most ghastly event to ever scar the history of the human race. And we have proof that it occurred. We have numerous accounts of witnesses, photographs of mass killings and mass burials, documentation of the high-level orders to proceed with the killings, statistics documenting the abrupt loss of millions of people, and more. Our proof couldn't be better.

> *Bob:* That's all rubbish! There is no proof that the Holocaust actually occurred. No one has ever produced a letter from God saying it happened. So, until I see that letter, don't talk to me about a Holocaust.

> *Rick:* But what about the witnesses' accounts, the photographs, and all the rest? Do you deny they exist?

> *Bob:* No, but they're not proof. The only real proof would have to come from God. God has not said that the Holocaust occurred, so there is no proof it did.

In this dispute Rick is using the word *proof* according to ordinary criteria, but Bob is not. In everyday English, when we speak of a past event being proven, we mean just the sorts of things that Rick lists (witnesses' accounts, photos). But the criterion that Bob uses is highly unusual. (Bob employs a metaphysical term that introduces a host of new concerns, which are discussed below.) Of course, he is free to do this; there is no law against inventing his own definitions of words. But it is highly misleading for him to say that there is no proof, because when he says this, his listeners are naturally going to apply the ordinary definition of that word. (We could predict this from basic principle 4.) It would cause much less confusion if Bob simply invented a new word with this new meaning instead of attaching a new meaning to an old word.

Rick and Bob not only differ over definitions, but Bob is inventing an entirely new definition that bears no resemblance to its usual meaning. Thus, it is irrelevant and highly misleading for Bob to say that there is no proof. Bob's trick of redefining words in no way refutes Rick's claim.

Multiple Meanings

Many confusions and pointless controversies can be avoided by simply taking into account the different criteria that people employ in speaking. In the context of science, for example, *work* means a force applied over a distance. This is not the criterion ordinarily employed for this word, and hence the meaning is different. It would be just a bad joke to tell two soldiers who had to stand very still on guard duty that they were doing no work. Similarly, in law the word *murder* is defined in a very technical way, so that euthanasia is considered to be murder. But in ordinary English the word *murder* is not invariably applied to all cases of euthanasia.

Another case in point is the word *theory*. When scientists speak of a theory, as in "the theory of evolution," they are speaking of an explanatory hypothesis well supported by evidence. When you and I use the word *theory* in everyday life, in contrast, we frequently mean an explanatory hypothesis based on little or no evidence whatsoever. Confusion arises when it is said (as it often is) that evolution is just a theory. Here, one criterion is substituted for another, and the false idea is created that the scientific theory of evolution is just a guess.

A final important example of confusion stemming from different criteria is what people do with the word *know*. Consider the following uses:

Bob: I know it's raining. [He has just come in from outside.]

Mary: I know it's raining. [She is inside the same building as Bob, and Bob has just phoned her and told her it's raining.]

Sharon: I know it's raining. [She is also inside the building, but she has heard nothing from Bob or Mary. Instead, she has suddenly gotten a strong feeling, which she calls intuition, that it's raining.]

These three uses of the word *know* are all fairly common, and the speakers are not breaking any rules of English. All three people use the same word, and this creates the illusion that they all mean the same thing. But the differences in these uses are quite important. (Whose testimony would you trust the most?) Each use has its own criteria, and they are significantly different. The meaning of the word in each case is, accordingly, different.

Confusion arises when someone, like Sharon, later says, "I *knew* it was raining!" (She becomes emphatic when firsthand investigation shows that she was right. You can be sure, however, that she, at that time, would not have been willing to bet her paycheck on her feeling.) She would like to think that her claim has as much authority as Bob's. But this is an illusion created by the fact that attention is not paid to the different criteria (the different meanings) employed.

ESP   The philosophical extension of Sharon's idea is that we have other ways of knowing things (intuition or extrasensory perception) besides the five senses. Here we have another example of an illusion created (at least in part, if not wholly) by language. If we had a different word specially reserved for cases like Sharon's and if we didn't ever use *know* in such cases, there would probably be no temptation to confuse Sharon's case with Bob's.

Truth   *Truth* is another word often used with different criteria. Consider:

>   *A:* I've found the truth. [said by a person who is devoted to a religious practice involving meditation exercises]

>   *B:* I've found the truth. [said by person who has just entered a group marriage]

>   *C:* I've found the truth. [said by a detective assigned to a murder case]

The criterion for the word *truth* in statement A is a special state of consciousness involving unique feelings or emotions. It may be a subjective state of mind that one must work hard to attain and that may be difficult, if not impossible, to explain to others. In statement B the criterion for the word *truth* is a lifestyle that meets the person's social, economic, and sexual needs. In statement C, on the other hand, the criterion for the word *truth* is the discovery that someone is lying or hiding something, a discovery that can be objectively demonstrated to a jury. The differences between these three uses (meanings) of the word *truth* are very great, and there are many other uses of the word as well.

When we realize that this word has a multitude of meanings, we can see that the question

What is *truth?*

is quite unclear. We cannot even attempt an answer until we know what meaning is intended. A wise person once said:

An unclear question has an infinite number of answers.

Because we don't really know what we're asking by the question "What is truth?" we can respond with whatever sounds good, and different people, of course, will have different answers. Considering our first three basic principles, the best way of answering this question would be to say that people use the word *truth* in a variety of ways and that therefore the word has a variety of meanings.

If we think that truth is a mystery because people disagree with its definition, we are succumbing to linguistic superstition once again.

❑ Chapter Review Questions

1. What are the four basic principles for understanding the nature of human language?
2. Define linguistic superstition.
3. We apply certain words according to criteria. Explain what criteria are. Give an example.
4. If, in applying a word, you use a special set of criteria instead of the ordinary ones, what consequences should you expect?
5. If you change the criteria for a word, you change the _____ of the word.
6. Give an example of a verbal dispute, and explain why it is verbal.
7. Give an example of a factual dispute, and explain why it is factual.
8. If you find yourself in a verbal dispute, how should you deal with it?
9. How are factual disputes settled?
10. What is a pseudomystery, and how does it differ from a real mystery?
11. Explain how a pseudomystery can be produced by linguistic superstition.

12. Based on what you've learned in this chapter, analyze the following argument:
    We all have our own idea of what beauty is, and these ideas are all different. This shows that no one really knows what beauty is.
13. Based on what you've learned inside and outside of this chapter, how would you respond to the following argument?
    Mental telepathy must be real, because otherwise we wouldn't have a word for it.

❏ Chapter Exercises

Decide whether each of the following disagreements is factual or verbal. If it is factual, say what observations can settle it. If it is verbal, identify the key term and state the different criteria employed by each disputant. The answers are given in the back of the book.

1. Mary: Leon Snodgrass is educated. In 1981 he graduated from Purdue University with a degree in business law, and since that time he has taken on over 150 cases.

   Ellen: Leon Snodgrass is not educated at all! Ask him any question about math or science or literature, and he won't be able to answer it. Sure, he knows all about law, but that doesn't make him educated.

2. Joslyn: The human embryo, even at the age of 14 days, has developed fingers and toes. My philosophy teacher told us that.

   Jake: That's not true. At that point (14 days after conception) the embryo doesn't even have limbs. You can look that up in any competent biology textbook.

3. Trish: My dog is intelligent, and I can prove it. Watch him. He can fetch the newspaper when I say, "Paper!" He shakes hands and rolls over, and he brings me his leash when he wants to go out for a walk.

   Tony: I disagree. Your dog is merely well-trained. He can't read, write, or solve math problems, so he's not intelligent.

4. Trudy: Homosexuality is not natural, because the people who practice it represent a very small minority within the total population.

Mabel: But look at other animals. You often see male dogs mounting each other. That proves that homosexuality is natural.

5. Ted: Obesity is sometimes caused by genetics. In other words, people can be born with the tendency to store fat. So regardless of how little they eat, they will be fat.

Matt: That's not true. All fat people are fat because they eat too much.

6. Stan: If a tree falls in the forest where no one (no conscious being) is present to hear it, it makes no sound. There can be no such thing as a sound that is not heard.

Millie: Absurd! What does the presence of conscious beings have to do with it? I'm sure it makes a hell of a sound whether there's anybody around to hear it or not. You could even make a tape recording of it, and a tape records sound.

7. Nate: Humanism is a religion, because it is a set of beliefs about reality and about how people should conduct their lives.

Connie: You're wrong. Humanism is *not* a religion, because it doesn't embrace a belief in a supreme being.

8. Leon: Abraham Lincoln was a Catholic even though he didn't attend church on a regular basis.

Kevin: No, Lincoln wasn't a Catholic. He was born a Presbyterian and remained one until he died.

9. Kate: The movie *Deep Throat* shows explicit sexual acts, and it should be banned because it's obscene.

Mort: What's wrong with the movie? The actors do nothing in that movie that millions of people don't do every day and night throughout the world without causing any harm to anyone. To call that obscene is to call life itself obscene. If you want to see something really obscene, go look at some videos of people getting blown apart in the war in Vietnam.

10. Steve: The United States is a democracy, because the ultimate power of governing is retained by the people.

Bruno: Actually, the United States is not a democracy, because the people do not govern themselves but are governed by elected representatives.

11. Scientist 1: Viruses are living things, because they are made up of DNA (genetic) material, and they invade living cells and use those cells to produce more viruses.

    Scientist 2: Viruses are not living things, because they cannot reproduce themselves, and they cannot manufacture enzymes or any other proteins.

12. Gerald: Hitler is dead. He committed suicide, and his charred body was found toward the end of World War II.

    Vivian: That's what most people think. But actually Hitler isn't dead. He escaped to South America, where he's been living since the war ended.

13. Drake: Paul is in the hospital, but he isn't dead. His heart is still beating, and his lungs are still breathing.

    Glenda: Yes, but he has a flat EEG. This means that his brain is no longer functioning. Paul is dead.

14. Henry: Gandhi was a true Christian, because he believed in peace and justice through passive resistance.

    Conrad: Gandhi was not a true Christian at all, because he didn't believe that Jesus was the only true son of God.

CHAPTER 2

❏ ❏ ❏ ❏ ❏ ❏ ❏

What Are We Saying?

It is wrong to say that good language is *important* to good thought, merely; for it is the essence of it.

Charles Sanders Peirce

In the previous chapter we saw how certain problems could arise from a failure to understand the nature and function of language. Now we'll turn to another type of linguistic pitfall: a failure to recognize and distinguish the different kinds of jobs we employ words and statements to do. Here is where linguistic illusions abound, because one use of language can look much like another.

❏ Word Types

Let's begin by elucidating four of the types of words we use:

1. descriptive words
2. value words
3. exclamations
4. metaphysical words

Clearly, this is not an exhaustive list. We are limiting our discussion to those types of words that pertain, directly or indirectly, to our main subject: thinking about science and the paranormal.

Descriptive Words

One of the most common uses that we make of words is *to describe our experiences*. A descriptive word is any word that we can teach to others by directing their attention to something that they can experience with the five senses (seeing, hearing, smelling, tasting, and feeling). Some of these words are simple and concrete, like *chair, cat, furry,* and *sitting;* others are more removed from our direct experience, like *intelligent, fragile,* and *Christianity.* The word *cat* can be taught by simply pointing to a cat, but the word *intelligent* cannot, because it describes the tendency of people or animals to act in certain ways. It can, nevertheless, be taught by showing. The word *Christianity* is even more general and is used to summarize a great deal of our experiences in a convenient form. It means the beliefs and practices of Christians, and these can be taught by showing.

From these examples you can see that many descriptive words are not used to describe our direct observations or immediate experiences. Many scientific words are like this. When we speak of an electron, we are not talking of something we can experience directly: all we can see is the way in which our measuring equipment behaves under certain circumstances. The term *gravity* is another example. We observe objects being attracted to each other, but strictly speaking, we do not observe something called gravity. We do not observe electrons or gravity in the same way that we observe billiard balls or falling bodies, but the meaning of these terms is still explained in terms of experience.

Many names for legendary creatures that have never been seen are also descriptive, for example, bigfoot or the Loch Ness monster. Of course, we can't present these animals to people to teach them the words, but we can show them pictures and models, and we can point to creatures similar in form.

Value Words

The purpose of a value word is to *evaluate.* In other words, we use value words to praise or blame, commend or criticize. Examples are *good, bad, right, wrong, virtuous, evil, better, worse,* and *great.* In applying these words to something, we are not describing it; we are judging it. If I say that Alfred is a good man, you know that my appraisal is positive, but I have given you no descriptive information about him. If I say that Alfred is a tall man, on the other hand, then I have told you something about him, because *tall* is a descriptive term.

You and I can both agree in calling Alfred a good man, but we might have radically different criteria for saying so. We both commend him, but I may be interested in Alfred's ability to play quarterback, whereas you may be interested in his ability to keep a conversation going. When we evaluate someone or something, we always do so according to some criteria that function as our standards of judging. We are not compelled to have in mind any particular criterion, but we must have some descriptive criteria. Hence, when I say that Alfred is a good man, you can naturally ask, "Why do you think so?" and my answer will be a listing of my criteria.

Most words that we use to evaluate already contain a descriptive element. In other words, they are *mixtures* of evaluation and description. *Murder* is a mixture word that describes an act of taking a human life and judges it as wrong. We do not call the act of swatting flies murder precisely because we do not judge it to be wrong. You can kill a fly, but you cannot murder one. *Stealing* is another example. Calling an act stealing is to do two things: (1) it describes the act as taking what belongs to another, and (2) it judges it as wrong. Other examples are *courageous, foolhardy, rash,* and *considerate.* These words describe a certain kind of act and also judge it. For example, *courageous* describes an act as one involving risk and judges it as good, and *foolhardy* describes an act as one involving risk but judges it as bad.

Since mixture words contain a value judgment, they should be handled with care when debating moral issues. If I believe that abortion is wrong, for instance, I cannot logically support my belief by saying that it is murder. This would be begging the question, because the word *murder* means "wrong." Thus, to say that "abortion is wrong because it's murder" is equivalent to saying that "abortion is wrong because it's wrong." A reason has not yet been given for saying that it is wrong. (See the fallacy of begging the question, in Chapter 3.)

Exclamations

An exclamation occurs when we use a word or words to express our feelings. If a man is shocked at what he sees, he may say, "Good God!" But in doing this he is not actually referring to God or praising him. It would be a mistake to take him literally here. He is really expressing a feeling of amazement, surprise, or shock. Many exclamations are just as expressive but could not possibly be interpreted descriptively. "Yipes!" "Golly!" and "Wow!" are examples.

When we use language to exclaim, we are *showing* our feelings rather than describing them. "I love you!" when said by a young man to his new wife in a sexual embrace is a verbal display of his feelings, not a description of them. (Hence, she would only be making a cruel joke if she replied, "Be more specific.")

Metaphysical Words

The word *metaphysical* means "beyond the physical." We use metaphysical words to talk about phenomena that (we believe) exist in an unseen or undetectable realm. Examples are *God, the soul, ghost, spirit, heaven,* and *astral plane.* The metaphysical concept of the soul as something immortal and immaterial that can detach itself from the body, for example, has never been given descriptive criteria. For this reason it lacks descriptive meaning. We do not apply it descriptively. That is, the use of the word *soul* does not depend on our having had certain experiences.

Compare this word with a descriptive word like *chair.* We call something a chair only if what we see meets the demands established by our criteria: Does it have four legs? Yes. Does it have a seat? Yes. Does it have a back? Yes. Is it made to hold one person? Yes. Is it made for sitting on? Yes. Seeing these conditions met, we can now apply to it the word *chair.* But this is not how we go about applying the word *soul* metaphysically. (Of course, the word can be used in other ways, too—for example: "the saxophonist plays with soul.")

We can speak of metaphysical criteria for the application of a metaphysical word, but they must be sharply distinguished from descriptive criteria. For example, we could say that (for many people) the criteria for applying the word *God* are "creator of the universe," "all-powerful," "eternal," and "infinitely good." Because we cannot specify precisely what experiences we are describing by these words, however, we cannot count them as descriptive criteria. If we could do this, the word *God* would be a descriptive word.

Statement Types

Now that we have briefly distinguished some different uses of words, we are in a better position to recognize important differences in the statements we make. This is extremely important if we are to accurately understand what a person is saying.

A *statement* can be defined as *a linguistic attempt to assert what is the case.* Because we are extremely interested in what is the case, assessing statements accurately is vitally important to us. In the rest of this chapter we will examine five types of statements, in order to distinguish them and understand their different functions:

1. empirical
2. analytic

3. value
4. attitude
5. metaphysical

❏ Empirical Statements

The word *empirical* is derived from the Greek word *empeiria,* meaning "sense experience." So let's define an *empirical statement* as one that *purports to convey information about the world of our sense experience,* past, present, or future. In other words, an empirical statement tells us something about the people, things, and events we see, hear, smell, taste, and feel. Here's an example:

There is a clock on the wall in the kitchen.

This statement is telling us something about the world of our five senses. It is saying that if we go into the kitchen and look on the wall, we will find a clock there. This is the mark of an empirical statement: *it tells us what sense experiences we will have if it is true or false.* Thus, it conveys empirical meaning to us. If we go into the kitchen and see that there is indeed a clock on the wall, the statement "There is a clock on the wall in the kitchen" is true (verified). And if we go into the kitchen and see that there is no clock on the wall, the statement is false (falsified). Obviously, the only way of finding out whether an empirical statement is true or false is by going and looking (experiencing).

If the statement is true, we could make it false by merely removing the clock from the wall. And if it's false, we could make it true by putting a clock on the wall. Every empirical statement is sensitive to the facts of experience in this way precisely because it conveys information about those facts. Hence, *the truth value of an empirical statement (that is, whether it is true or false) is determined by observed facts.*

Other Characteristics of an Empirical Statement

Descriptive Words Are Required Notice the connection between empirical statements and descriptive words: *empirical statements need descriptive words. Clock, on, wall,* and *kitchen* are all words for which we have descriptive criteria. In other words, we know what it's like to experience these things with our five senses. This is why the statement conveys empirical information (meaning) to us. Now look what happens if we substitute a nondescriptive word for one of the important descriptive words:

There is a trindalian on the wall in the kitchen.

(I have just now made up the word *trindalian,* and I have not yet given it a definition.) The word *trindalian* conveys no descriptive information to you, and consequently, you do not know what experiences you will have if the statement is true or false. Going into the kitchen and looking will do you no good, because you do not know what to look for. Even if the kitchen were empty, you would still not know whether the statement was true or false. Thus, the statement with the word "trindalian" is empirically meaningless to you.

It Doesn't Need to Be True   When we call a statement empirical, we do not mean that it is true. Any empirical statement can be true or false depending on what the observed facts happen to be. If we walked into the kitchen and found no clock on the wall, our statement would be false, but it would still be empirical. What makes it empirical is that we know what the kitchen will look like if it is true or false. *It does not need to be true* to be empirical.

It would also be a mistake to think that an empirical statement is one that is proven. *Lots of empirical statements are not proven.* For example, the statement "Bigfoot exists" has never been proven, but we have descriptive criteria for the word *bigfoot* (a primate, 8 to 10 feet tall, weighing 500 to 800 pounds, covered with hair, standing erect). Therefore, we know what experiences we will have if the statement is true or false. It is empirically meaningful.

Many paranormal claims are empirical in spite of the fact that rigorous scientific evidence for them is lacking. Some examples are:

Some people can read other people's thoughts (mental telepathy).

Some people can bend spoons with their minds (psychokinesis).

Some people can see through brick walls (clairvoyance).

Our planet is being visited by creatures from distant worlds
(extraterrestrials).

Each of these statements is empirical, because we know what experiences we will have if it is true or false.

It Doesn't Need to Be Provable A statement can be empirical even though we lack the necessary means to prove it true or false. Consider this example:

> There is a planet in the M1 galaxy with a mountain on it over 50 miles high.

This galaxy is millions of light-years away, too far for us to investigate. But the statement is still empirical, because we know what experiences we *will* have if it is true or false. In other words, if we could get there, we would know what to look for. *We do not need to be able to prove a statement for it to be empirical.*

Vague Statements

Many statements that are thought to be empirical actually are not because of their vagueness. For example, I was told by someone who was supposed to be a psychic that I had "recently made an important change." Now, if this is an empirical statement, it is telling me what experiences I have had if it is true (or haven't had if it is false). I wondered: What does she mean by "important"? Important psychologically? physiologically? monetarily? socially? And which changes could she mean, for I've made a lot of them recently: I bought a car, changed my freeway route to work, changed my brand of toothpaste, resolved to smile to the grumpy person who sits behind the front desk at the personnel office, and decided to postpone a trip to the dentist. And what does she mean by "recently"? One week? One month? Two years? The longer I wondered about this, the more I realized I didn't know what experiences I was supposed to have had if her statement was true.

I also didn't know what it would be like for her statement to be false. Would it be false if the only change I'd made within the last two weeks was my brand of toothpaste? Doubtful, because perhaps this change would lead to something of greater significance, or perhaps I needed to look at the past three weeks instead of just the past two. The point is, I did not know what experiences, if any, would have been incompatible with her statement.

Because I did not know what experiences I was supposed to have had or not have had, the psychic's statement was empirically meaningless. That is to say, it may have seemed as if she were saying something about me, but she actually wasn't.

Weasel Words   Another way to make a statement vague and thereby destroy its empirical meaning is to put a "weasel word" into it. Some examples of weasel words are *may, might, perhaps, can,* and *could*. The term *weasel word* derives from the wily animal that can poke a hole in an egg and suck out the contents, leaving a hollow shell. Likewise, when a weasel word appears in a statement, it extracts any definite meaning that the statement would otherwise have. For instance, if someone says, "You have an allergy to cheese," this remark is empirically meaningful (you know what experiences you will have if it's true and what experiences you will have if it's false). But if someone says, "You might have an allergy to cheese," the word *might* adds so much vagueness that falsifiability is impossible, making the statement empirically meaningless.

This device is often employed by psychic readers, because it creates a "can't-lose" situation for them: if you have an allergy to cheese, the reader can call this a hit. If you don't have an allergy to cheese, the reader doesn't have to count this a miss, because he or she only said that you *might* have an allergy to cheese.

Meaningful Vagueness   Of course, not all vague statements are empirically meaningless. Suppose I say to you, "Drake is a tall man." I am not saying how tall, and you might wonder, "How tall is 'tall'?" I could mean 5 feet 11 inches, 6 feet 2, or 7 feet 3. But nonetheless, you can be quite certain that I don't mean that Drake is under 3 feet tall. The statement, though vague, is still falsifiable and, therefore, empirically meaningful.

The Importance of Falsifiability

In a brochure for a psychic fair held in San Diego on May 23 and 24, 1987, there was a list of suggestions entitled "Hints for a Good Reading." There were 14 hints, and number 7 said: "Do not be quick to say 'no.' Wait . . . you will soon understand." So if the reader's statement seems false, that means you haven't given yourself enough time to find some way to make it fit. Clearly, this rule makes any statement by the reader immune to falsification. Consequently, any such statement is empirically meaningless, because verifiability and falsifiability are two sides of the same coin: you can't have one without the other. *A statement that lacks falsifiability also lacks verifiability*. Think of it this way: a statement that excludes nothing includes nothing.

Such examples of people playing with words are actually quite common. Statements sound empirical, and the people who make them intend them as such. But lack of falsifiability shows these statements to be devoid of empirical meaning.

Let's now summarize the four main characteristics of an empirical statement:

1. It is used to convey information about the world that we experience with our five senses.
2. It tells us what experiences we'll have if it's true (verifiability).
3. It tells us what experiences we'll have if it's false (falsifiability).
4. It is true or false depending on observed facts.

❑ Analytic Statements

Some of our statements do not describe facts that we can experience but, instead, they *speak only about words.* "All bachelors are unmarried" is an example of such an *analytic statement.* This statement is true, not because of the facts but because of the words. The word *bachelor means* unmarried. Thus, the statement is true by (human-made) definition because the meaning of the predicate (*are unmarried*) is already contained in the subject (*bachelor*).

The big difference between empirical statements and analytic statements is that empirical statements tell us about the world available to our five senses, but analytic statements tell us only about the meaning of words. Analytic statements tell us nothing about the empirical world and have *no empirical meaning.*

This might sound strange, because the statement "All bachelors are unmarried" certainly seems to be about things we can experience, namely, bachelors. But remember, any statement that describes facts could be true or false depending on what the facts happen to be. Now, can we imagine arranging the facts to make this statement false? Let's try the following thought experiment: all bachelors in the world suddenly get married! Would our statement then be false? No, because now those men would no longer be bachelors. In other words, if a man were married, we would not (in ordinary English) call him a bachelor. Thus, there is simply no way of manipulating the facts in the world of our experience in such a way that our statement "All bachelors are unmarried" would be false. This means that our statement is not about the facts in the world perceived by our five senses. *If no sense experiences could verify or falsify a statement, that statement is simply not about the world we experience with our five senses.* Now let's look at some other examples:

A mother has a child.

Shoes are worn on the feet.

Tomorrow is the day after today.

All men are human beings.

A puppy is a young dog.

These statements are all true, but they tell us nothing about the world that we experience with our five senses. They are not true by observed fact; they are *true by definition.* They tell us only about how certain words are used in English. They may look as if they were conveying factual information, but this is just a linguistic illusion. If they were telling us something about observed facts, it would be possible to make them false by changing the facts. But these statements would still be true no matter what the facts happened to be. The statement "A puppy is a young dog" looks as if it were talking about puppies, but it isn't. It is true regardless of what might happen to puppies, even if they were all destroyed.

The fact that analytic statements look grammatically just like empirical statements is one of the common pitfalls of language. For example, the statement "God created the universe" is analytically true if the word *God* is defined (as it frequently is) as "the creator of the universe." Hence, the statement is really saying "The creator of the universe created the universe."

A great deal of confusion develops within discussions and debates when an analytic statement is asserted to be an empirical one. Consider the following dialogue:

Clint: God created the universe.

Clovis: What do you mean by "God"? Define your term.

Clint: God is the all-powerful, all-knowing, benevolent, eternal creator of all that is.

Clovis: But how do you know the universe got started that way?

> *Clint:* Because God *is* the creator. He wouldn't be God if He hadn't created the universe.

We can see that what Clint *means* by *God* is "the creator of the universe." He also thinks he is saying something about the world we experience, but actually he is merely defining his word. His statement is true by definition, and for this reason it tells us nothing factual about the world of our experience. The statement "Unicorns have one horn" is also true by definition, but it tells us nothing about experiences that we will or will not have with our five senses. And it does not tell us that unicorns exist.

Tautologies and Contradictions

If a statement can be true by definition, a statement can also be false by definition. For example, because "All bachelors are unmarried" is true by definition, "All bachelors are married" is false by definition. A statement that is true by definition is called a *tautology* (Greek: *tautos* = "same"; *logos* = "word"), and a statement that is false by definition is called a *contradiction* (Latin: *contra* = "against"; *dictio* = "saying"). In a tautology the predicate merely repeats the subject, but in a contradiction the predicate negates the subject. Whereas a tautology is redundant and merely defines a term, a contradiction is saying nothing at all, because the information given in the subject is withdrawn in the predicate.

Paradoxes

This last point is important to remember when we come upon paradox in reasoning. A paradox is any verbal construction that is contradictory or entails a contradiction. Take, for example, the notion of a square circle. What is a square circle? Listen to the following definition:

> **square circle:** a two-dimensional plane figure enclosed by four equal straight lines, having four right angles, and making a figure that has no straight lines but is enclosed by a continuous curved line such that all points are equidistant from the center

Got it? Of course you can't get it, because the definition contains a contradiction ("enclosed by four equal straight lines . . . and . . . has no straight lines"). This is the mark of a paradoxical idea: there is nothing to get, because nothing is given. I first gave you four straight lines, and then I promptly took them back. That leaves you with a grand total of nothing. What you are left with is a meaningless jumble of words that defies comprehension because it is saying nothing. A paradox, because it is contradictory, makes no sense. In other words, to speak of a square circle, as I have defined it, is rather like babbling gibberish.

Now let's look at a subtler example of a paradox:

> In a small village all the men are clean-shaven. Each man either shaves himself or is shaven by a certain male barber in this village, who shaves only those men who do not shave themselves.

A little reflection shows that the above paragraph is paradoxical, because it entails a contradiction. We can see the contradiction if we ask this question: Does the barber shave himself, or does someone else shave him? If he does shave himself, then he doesn't! And if he doesn't, then he does! Trying to imagine these possibilities boggles the mind, but it would be a mistake born of linguistic superstition to think that the difficulty is intrinsic to the case or that we simply lack the necessary mental equipment to deal with it.

The problem is not that we lack the intelligence to comprehend the situation (of the barber) but that we, in creating it, have made some kind of mistake. If we think the paradox of the barber must describe a real possibility that lies beyond our powers of understanding, we are being taken in by linguistic superstition. (For a further illustration, see the Appendix, item 1.) We are forgetting that words, word combinations, and the meaning (or nonsense) that results are human creations (basic principle 1).

So what's to be done? In everyday life, when somebody points out our contradictions, we respond (or ought to respond) very reasonably: we revise our statement. It should be the same in every case of a paradox: we created it, so we can undo it. Because a paradox is a piece of unintelligible verbiage that we have created in the act of defining or combining words, we should take responsibility for it and redefine or recombine our words to form an intelligible message.

Our mistake in the barber paradox is in putting concepts (words) together that are incompatible. We can give up the idea of all the townsmen being clean-shaven, we can have the barber reside in a neighboring village, or we can make the barber a woman. But something must be changed. The paradox is a certain indication that we have broken our own linguistic rules.

Many discussions about God also involve paradoxes. Here are two of them:

God existed before time existed.

God exists outside of space.

These are paradoxical statements because the word *before* places God in time, and the word *outside* places God in space. In other words, "before time existed" is a contradiction, and "outside of space" is a contradiction.

But some theological paradoxes are not as easy to spot—for example, God's infinite power. The standard way of defining *infinite power* is to say that God can do anything at all. (Some would say that God can even perform a contradiction, and so He can make a square circle. See the Appendix, item 2.) At first this sounds quite reasonable, but it soon runs into problems. If God can do just anything, surely he can do anything you can do. You can make something so heavy you cannot lift it. Now let's suppose God, too, can make a rock so big He cannot lift it. If He can do this, then there is something He cannot do: lift that rock. On the other hand, if He cannot do this, again there is something He cannot do: make that rock. Either way, there is something God cannot do.

Thus, if we define God as an infinite power, we wind up with the following contradiction: there is something that can't be done by a being who can do anything! This shows that our linguistic rules forbid the combining of the word *infinite* with the word *power*. Notice that there is no problem when we combine the word *infinite* with the word *series,* as when we define 1, 2, 3, . . . as an infinite series of numbers. This just means that there is no highest number but that whatever number is selected can be increased by adding 1 to it.

It might seem that the question "Could God make a rock so big He couldn't lift it?" is just a verbal trick. It isn't. Consider what happens when you apply this question to a human power. Could you make a structure so big you couldn't lift it? The answer is yes, and no paradox results. But when we speak of an infinite power doing the same thing, we get something incoherent. This does not mean that we lack the brain power to grasp it. Rather, it means that we've got to go back to the drawing board and change the definitions or combinations of our terms in order to eliminate the paradox.

We might, for example, want to redefine *infinite* to mean not that there is nothing God cannot do but that whatever He can do, He can do it without limit. Or, we might want to replace *infinite* with *inconceivably great*. These are just two suggested solutions, and I'm sure there are more. But whichever way we go, we must do something to eliminate the paradox. We must not forget that the words *God, infinite,* and *power* are (like all other words) human inventions. Thus, the paradox is something that we have created.

One fairly common response to this paradox is to say that it is only a paradox for us, not for God. But to say this is to succumb to linguistic superstition; it is to regard words as something more than tools created by humans for the purpose of communication. It is also to miss the point that in a paradox we contradict ourselves, and when we contradict ourselves we say nothing at all.

Before we go on to the next type of statement, let's summarize the four main characteristics of an analytic statement:

1. It is true or false by definition (a tautology or a contradiction).
2. When true, it conveys information about words only.
3. When false, it conveys no information at all.
4. It has no empirical meaning.

❏ Value Statements

Value statements are assertions that involve value words like *good* and *bad, right* and *wrong, better* and *worse,* or *ought* and *ought not* and mixture words like *honest* and *dishonest, brave* and *cowardly,* or *kind* and *cruel.* We use these words when we wish to *praise, blame, condemn, or condone someone or something.* You will recall that these words are always used in connection with some descriptive criteria. These criteria give value statements *empirical meaning.* For example, suppose that I say "Joe is a kind person" and that my criteria for *kind* are:

1. being careful not to hurt other people's feelings
2. being willing to put oneself out for others

These criteria provide you with a means of verifying (or falsifying) my statement. If you observe Joe and see that he is careful not to hurt other people's feelings and is willing to put himself out for others, you know that my statement about Joe is true, given my criteria for the term *kind.* On the other hand, if you observe that Joe carelessly hurts other people's feelings and is not willing to put himself out for others, you know that my statement is false, relative to those same criteria.

In other words, a value statement is verifiable and falsifiable, just as an empirical statement is. Descriptive criteria make it possible for me (or anyone who knows my criteria) to investigate and discover whether my statement is true or false. Thus, in making a value statement, *we not only judge something, we also convey empirical information about it*.

But what happens when people have different criteria? Shall we just call it a verbal dispute and let it go at that? Not necessarily. Let's suppose that you know Joe, too, and you disagree with me, saying "Joe is *not* a kind person." And let's say your criteria for *kind* are:

1. being careful not to hurt other people's feelings
2. being willing to put oneself out for others
3. refusing to eat meat, because it means killing animals

We share the first two criteria but not the third. Joe is a meat eater, and therefore you judge him not to be a kind person. We have a verbal difference. This means that we could both be right, because *kind* means one thing to me and something else to you. Unless we share all the same criteria, it is impossible for either of us to win this argument.

But we need not stop here. I might try to convince you that my set of criteria is better than yours, and you might try to convince me that yours is better. But again, in order to do this we must agree on a higher criterion for evaluating our different sets of criteria. For example, we might come to agree that human happiness is a good criterion for judging a set of criteria. The question then becomes: whose criteria for *kind* produces more human happiness, yours or mine? And again, this question can be settled by observation when human happiness is defined descriptively.

I don't mean to suggest that this process is simple and easy but only that value disputes can often be resolved in an empirical way. Given that most human beings have the same ultimate needs and desires, we do have a basis for logically resolving many important differences in judgment.

In summary, the four characteristics of a value statement are:

1. It is used to judge something or someone.
2. It contains a value word or mixture word.
3. It is true or false depending on observed facts.
4. It has empirical meaning.

❏ Attitude Statements

Attitude statements are like exclamations in that *they tell us something about the speaker but tell us nothing at all about facts and events in the world we experience.* In other words, when people make attitude statements, they are telling us how they feel about things; they are not telling us something about those things. Thus, attitude statements are *empirically meaningless.* Attitude statements should be sharply distinguished from value statements. Both tell us something about how the speaker feels, but value statements are empirically meaningful, whereas attitude statements are not. In other words, a genuine value statement will be true or false depending on what's observed, but an attitude statement is not affected by any observed facts. For example, a bumper sticker I saw recently said:

> The worst day fishing is better than the best day working.

This statement really tells us nothing about fishing or about working, but it does tell us something about the person who made it: he or she strongly prefers fishing to working. And in this statement:

> Down with communism!

the speaker is not saying anything about communism but is letting us know that he or she isn't too keen on it.

Fraudulent Empirical Meaning

Problems arise when people make attitude statements that they think are empirical ones. For example, suppose Shane says:

> Toyota automobiles never break down.

It looks as if Shane were saying something empirical; that is, it looks as if he were saying something about the reliability of Toyotas. And he might be; it all depends on whether he allows falsifiability as well as verifiability. In other words, Shane must allow the possibility of certain observations counting *against* his statement, just as he allows the possibility of certain observations counting *for* it.

Suppose Shane points to lots of evidence for his claim but allows nothing to count against it. Let's say we ask Shane: "What if a Toyota owner got into his car and it wouldn't start, and later a Toyota mechanic diagnosed the problem as a defective fuel pump?" Or "What if the owner of a new Toyota finds herself stalled on the freeway and later learns that she needs a whole new engine?"

If Shane responds to all such "What if . . ." questions by making up excuses ("The owner didn't get it serviced properly," "The driver abused it," or "It must have been damaged in shipment"), we can rightly suspect that he is merely expressing his attitude about Toyotas while saying nothing informative about them. On the other hand, if Shane says that he would admit he's wrong if such cases could be found, his statement is empirically meaningful.

The Quick Test

There is a quicker way, however, to determine whether a statement that looks empirical is really just an attitude statement: ask the person who makes the statement this question:

Could anything change your mind?

This question gets directly to the issue of falsifiability. If the answer is no, the person is making an attitude statement, not an empirical one. In other words, if the speaker intends to stick to the claim regardless of any observed facts that might turn up, he or she is really not saying anything about the world of observed facts.

Now let's look at another example. Josh says:

All people are basically good.

This looks like a value statement with empirical significance; it looks as if it's telling us something about people. In fact, Josh could point to Abraham Lincoln and Florence Nightingale as shining examples of human goodness. So let's ask him if anything could falsify his statement. Was Hitler basically good? Was Attila the Hun basically good? And what about Charles Manson? If Josh says that these people were distorted by their family lives and that underneath their ugly exterior was a basically good person, it becomes impossible to imagine anything falsifying his statement. No matter how horrible a person might seem, Josh is still going to say that he or she is good underneath it all. Thus, his statement *is not falsifiable and therefore not empirical.*

This means that Josh is conveying no information about people at all; he is merely expressing his feelings about them. In order for a statement to be empirically meaningful, it must be sensitive to the facts of experience. Certain observations could make it true, and certain other observations could make it false. *If no conceivable observations could falsify the statement, it is telling us nothing about the world of our experience.* Josh's statement tells us something about him (his feelings), but it tells us absolutely nothing about anything or anyone else. But he certainly thinks it does.

This is an illusion of language that's quite common: people think that they are saying something factual about the world of people and things that we experience, when really they are doing nothing more than expressing their feelings about that world. It might look as if Josh's statement were factually significant, because he can point to Lincoln and Nightingale as confirming instances. But this is an illusion: *if no observations could refute a statement, no observations can confirm it either.*

Now let's look at an example from the paranormal. Many people believe that certain individuals have the psychic power to know things about us that they couldn't have known by any normal means. By just holding something of ours (a ring or a watch) or by just being in our presence, the gifted individual can "pick up" information about us. A friend of mine (we'll call her Ruth) told me that a psychic had said that Ruth had been married on a boat (true) and that her husband's name was Paul (true). Because Ruth had never met this man before, she became an instant believer, declaring: "Reginald Rios has psychic power."

Subsequently, however, Ruth's mother visited Rios and the results were disappointing. He was wrong about the number of her children, wrong about her birthplace, and wrong about her profession. Did this change Ruth's mind about Rios? Not a bit, because, Ruth explained, his gift is not constant. Sometimes he has it, and sometimes he doesn't. Perhaps. But a few months later, Ruth's brother, Tom, went to Rios for a reading and asked questions about a brother who, he said, wandered off three years earlier. "He's on the East Coast, unemployed, and lonely, but his health is good, and he is in no danger," said Rios. This was interesting, because Tom had no brother. And what did Ruth have to say about this? She said that sometimes a psychic will pick up information about someone else instead of the person spoken to. "Crossed vibes," she called it.

Since Ruth's imaginative mind spins out excuses without limit, it seems unlikely that anything could change her mind about Rios. This means that when Ruth says, "Reginald Rios has psychic power," her statement is unfalsifiable, and therefore she is merely expressing a feeling or attitude about him and not conveying any information about him. It may sound as if she were saying something about Rios, but she isn't.

A rather amusing example of an attitude statement was given to me by a student. He was told by an astrologer that his horoscope for that particular day was exceptionally positive. "Good things are going to happen to you today," she said. Later that same day, he was in an auto accident with his girlfriend. She was very seriously injured, and he had a few broken bones, too. Did this calamity falsify the astrologer's statement? Not a bit. She said to him, "A very good thing did happen to you: you're alive!" By the same "reasoning," if he had been killed, she could have said, "That was the best thing that could have happened to him: his problems are now over, and his quick death may have averted some horrible future torment."

The astrologer put herself in a "can't-lose" position: many things could support her statement, but nothing could disconfirm it. Because she permitted herself boundless freedom to defend what she said, she made it impossible to prove her wrong. Her statement was safe because it was unfalsifiable. But because it was unfalsifiable, it was empirically meaningless: it was actually conveying no information whatsoever about the world we experience. If no experiences can count against a statement, no experiences can count for it. Her statement expressed an attitude only.

Let's now summarize the five main characteristics of an attitude statement:

1. It is used to express the speaker's feelings.
2. It conveys information about the speaker only.
3. It can be mistaken for an empirical statement by both the speaker and the listener.
4. It lacks falsifiability (and, therefore, verifiability).
5. It has no empirical meaning.

❑ Metaphysical Statements

When we make a metaphysical statement, we are attempting to *assert a fact that cannot be observed*. Such statements often refer to a realm of being believed to lie beyond the five senses, a supernatural region existing outside of the natural order. This statement:

There is a God in heaven.

is a good example, because most people think of God and heaven as unavailable to our five senses. Here are a few more examples:

Humans possess an immortal soul.

There is life after death.

The physical world is merely an illusion of the mind.

The Ouija board works through the action of spirits.

There are seven astral planes.

The Jones house is haunted.

These statements, like all metaphysical statements, do not tell us what sense experiences we will have if they are true or false. And because they do not tell us about sense experience, metaphysical statements are, by definition, *empirically meaningless*. (If they were empirically meaningful, they would be empirical and not metaphysical.) This is neither bad nor good, it is simply the nature of the case. But we need to be clear about this fact if we are to avoid confusing metaphysical statements with empirical statements. Such a mistake could lead us to have inappropriate expectations.

Let me illustrate:

There is intelligent life in the Andromeda galaxy.

is an empirical statement that leads us to expect that someday we might know whether it is true or false. This is not a totally unreasonable expectation, because space travel is already here and because we have descriptive criteria for *intelligent life*. This means that we'll know it if we see it. But we cannot have similar expectations for the statement "There is life after death," because we don't know what sense experiences (or any other kind of experiences) we'll have if it is true or false.

Many people feel quite vague about the details of existence after death, but this, they say, is no reason to think that we won't experience it. Even though we cannot be sure what it will be like to go on "living" after we die, when it happens we will certainly know it.

But can this be so? Is it really possible to discover that a statement is true without knowing in advance what that experience would be like? Could we actually realize that we were dead without knowing how to tell? In other words, can we verify without descriptive guidelines (criteria)?

It seems that the answer to this question has to be no, because if I don't know what experiences I will have if the statement is true or false, I am left with no way of making the necessary determination. If I have no way at all of telling whether I'm dead, then for all I know, I'm dead right now! But this only illustrates that the statement "I am dead" is (when taken literally) empirically meaningless and that making an empirical discovery that I am dead is quite impossible. (Of course, I can always *believe* that I have made such a discovery.)

The problem with saying "We don't need descriptive criteria; we'll just know it when it happens" can be illustrated in the following way. Consider the statement "Trindalians exist." Now of course you don't know what a trindalian is, and you will ask me to describe it. To you I say: "I can't describe it, but when you see one, you'll just know it's a trindalian." You'll be immediately struck by the absurdity of this statement. If you have no descriptive clues at all, it's simply not true that you will recognize a trindalian when you see one. You can pick out certain experiences and choose to believe that they are the experiences of a trindalian, but you can't know whether they really are. (For further discussion of this topic, see the Appendix, item 3.)

James Kidd: Looking for Empirical Evidence of the Soul

Many people feel that this problem is simply a matter of ignorance and that as our knowledge grows, we will someday know what to look for to prove a metaphysical claim. In 1946, for example, an Arizona miner named James Kidd died and, in a hand-written will, left his estate to "research or [*sic*] some scientific proof of a soul of the human body which leaves at death." After a long period of probate his estate of $200,000 was finally awarded in 1973 to the American Society for Psychical Research.

Kidd believed that in the future there could be proof of a soul even though he was uncertain of what that proof would be like. "I think," he said in his will, "in time their can be a Photograph of soul [*sic*] leaving the human at death." But could Mr. Kidd (or anyone else) recognize a photograph of the soul leaving the body? How could a person tell whether a certain photograph was actually a photograph of the soul leaving the body or whether it was a photograph of something else? Can we correctly identify something without knowing what we are looking for? Can the advance of scientific knowledge help us here?

Let's look at the efforts made by the ASPR after it was awarded the $200,000. In a newsletter of July 1976 the society reported that, since 1973, it had been concentrating on two hypotheses: "that some part of the human personality is capable of operating outside the living body on rare occasions"—that is, a temporary out-of-body experience (OBE) —and "that it may continue to exist after the brain processes have ceased and the organism is decayed"—that is, life after death. Several projects were conducted. Subjects experienced apparitions that were compatible with the OBE hypothesis, but, the ASPR admitted, other explanations were possible (for example, ESP). Experiments with mediums and photographs yielded negative results. As for the second hypothesis, death-bed studies of apparitions, visions, and hallucinations strongly suggested that the patient was glimpsing out-of-body existence. But again, the ASPR said, other interpretations could not be ruled out.

Does the ASPR know what to look for in its attempt to prove that the soul exists? It seems not, because the phenomena it observed were, it admitted, susceptible to different interpretations. What, then, *would* indicate the presence or absence of the soul? I've heard it said that at the moment of death a person loses 1/3,000th of an ounce of body weight. If this is true, would it prove the existence of the soul? No, because this (doubtful) claim has other interpretations. No matter what is offered as evidence, it is always subject to alternative explanations and therefore does not constitute compelling proof of the soul.

The problem is that we simply have not decided what experiences constitute actual proof of the soul. (This is because we have not made *soul* a descriptive word.) And until we decide this, waiting for proof to come along is futile. Waiting for proof of any metaphysical claim is like waiting for proof of a trindalian. We simply do not know what we are waiting for. Of course, we can choose to *believe* that some phenomena prove the existence of the soul, if we feel like doing so. This is a personal matter of belief or faith that each individual is entitled to. But choosing to believe that we have proof is not the same as really having proof.

In the final analysis metaphysical statements cannot be given empirical proof, simply because they are not empirical. Metaphysical statements are in a class by themselves, and we should not expect of them what we expect of empirical statements. Nor should we call them meaningless just because they don't have empirical meaning. They have their own type of meaning: metaphysical meaning.

Nonempirical Experiences

We should also observe that humans are capable of far more than just empirical experiences. Some of our most important experiences are not of the empirical sort. For example, we experience feelings like belonging, intimacy, kindness, dread, alienation, and rejection; we experience emotions like love, hate, and fear; and we experience dreams. These are not sense experiences, and they can profoundly affect our lives. Some people are impressed by the out-of-body experience; they really do have it, and this is not a sense experience. There can be no denying, also, that many people do have experiences that they call the experience of God. These experiences are common enough to say that all people probably do have them or, at least, are capable of having them.

I, myself, have had an out-of-body experience more than once. The time I remember most vividly was when I went, at age eight, to have my tonsils taken out. I remember the mask being put over my face and then the intense smell of oranges (ether). The next thing I knew, I was floating above the operating table and looking down at myself surrounded by people wearing surgical gowns and gloves. It was a rather dreamlike experience and did not seem strange at the time, but after the operation I thought about it with great curiosity.

Much later in life I had what I would call religious experiences. In other words, there were moments when I felt I was an integral part of an infinite, all-encompassing power. For example, as I was watching the sun set from a 9,000-foot peak in Yosemite National Park, I was filled with a profound feeling of peace and contentment. I saw the universe as unutterably beautiful and perfect, and the problems and fears that normally occupy my mind became laughably insignificant. All things and all events seemed right and proper just as they were: they belonged, as part of the perfect whole. This was an enormously satisfying experience, and I still have experiences of this kind on occasion. It's also an experience that some would call the experience of God.

The Value of Metaphysical Statements

Many of the experiences that give our lives depth and meaning find expression in metaphysical statements, and the fact that they lack empirical meaning in no way detracts from their power to benefit us. Believing that God exists or that the soul is immortal can give comfort to the present and add hope to the future.

But there are dangers, too. It is a tragic waste of our limited resources to invest time, money, and energy in seeking proof from the empirical sciences of a metaphysical claim. And when a dispute between people or nations rests ultimately on different metaphysical assumptions, the possibility of resolution is beyond the scope of the empirical sciences, because these disciplines require descriptive terms, and they attempt to verify only empirical claims. A clear understanding of the unempirical status of metaphysical ideas should be salutary. If someone embraces metaphysical ideas different from ours, this is not a good reason for animosity, and to kill because of such differences seems to border on insanity.

Let us now summarize the main characteristics of a metaphysical statement:

1. It is used to talk about a supposed realm of being not perceived by the five senses (that is, it has metaphysical meaning).
2. It does not tell us what sense experiences we will have if it is true or what sense experiences we will have if it is false (that is, it lacks empirical meaning).

❏ What Are We Saying?

It is important to properly identify or classify a statement as empirical, analytic, value, attitude, or metaphysical, but we have to realize that often we actually cannot do this just by looking at the words. We need to ask speakers questions in order to determine how they are using their words. For example, if they say, "Tom is a good person," they are probably making a value statement, but they may be making an attitude statement. It all depends on whether they allow falsifiability or not. Or if they say, "God exists," they are probably speaking metaphysically, but not necessarily. They could be speaking empirically, analytically, attitudinally, or metaphysically (or none of the above). Any of these is possible. If they provide descriptive criteria for the word *God,* they are making an empirical statement. If they define God as existence itself (as many pantheists do), the statement "God exists" becomes analytic, that is, true by definition. If they point to certain objects of sense experience as verifying their claim but would allow no experiences of any kind to count against it, they are making an attitude statement. And if they decline to give descriptive criteria for God and assert that we have, as yet, no means of verifying it or falsifying it, they are speaking metaphysically.

Thus, we can see that it's impossible to categorize a statement at a glance. We cannot know what kind of statement people are making without having certain information about how they are using their words. This is not surprising, because, as we saw earlier, words do not have meaning in and of themselves. The meaning of a word or statement depends on what people do with it (basic principle 2).

The value of developing a consciousness of language cannot be overestimated. People fight and die over words with doubtful meaning and over statements with no clear descriptive content. If we train ourselves to think about what we are trying to do with our words, much controversy, confusion, and conflict can be avoided. We should constantly ask ourselves: What am I trying to do with these words? Am I asserting something about a fact that people can witness with their sense organs (empirical)? Am I saying something that conveys information merely about words (analytic)? Am I making a judgment about something with verifiable reasons for it (value)? Am I merely expressing my feelings about something (attitude)? Am I asserting something that could never be verified by sense experience but that might be significant in an entirely different way (metaphysical)?

Language is often taken for granted as something that needs no special attention. In reality, the difference between clear thinking and muddled thinking frequently lies in a sensitivity to words and their uses. We cannot make intellectual or moral progress if we are spinning our wheels in a verbal dispute, trying to refute a tautology, or looking for evidence to verify or falsify an attitude statement or a metaphysical statement.

Realizing the actual function of a word or statement can also go a long way toward reducing tension and averting hostilities. Human history offers countless examples of blood shed over issues that are fundamentally verbal, attitudinal, or metaphysical and that are empirically meaningless. In all probability awareness of language could have prevented many of them.

❏ Chapter Review Questions

1. Define descriptive words. Give examples.
2. Define value words. Give examples.
3. Define exclamatory words. Give examples.
4. Define metaphysical words. Give examples.
5. Explain why it is not appropriate to use mixture words when giving reasons for your moral judgments.

6. How can you tell when a person is making an empirical statement? Give an example.
7. How can you tell when a person is making an analytic statement? Give an example.
8. How can you tell when a person is making a value statement? Give an example.
9. How can you tell when a person is making an attitude statement? Give an example.
10. How can you tell when a person is making a metaphysical statement? Give an example.
11. Define tautology.
12. A false analytic statement is called a _____.
13. What is a paradox?
14. What role does linguistic superstition play in the production of a paradox?
15. When does a statement have empirical meaning?
16. Give an example of how a person can think that he is making a value statement when he is really just making an attitude statement.
17. Give an example of how a person can think that she is making an empirical statement when she is really just making an attitude statement.
18. Give an example of a false empirical statement.
19. Give an example of a false analytic statement.
20. How much information about the observable world can we learn from true analytic statements?
21. Can a value statement be proven? If so, how?
22. How can a metaphysical statement acquire empirical meaning?
23. What's wrong with saying, "A statement is empirical only if you can prove it"?
24. Give an example of an empirical statement that we cannot prove.
25. How could you transform a false empirical statement into a true one?
26. What is the problem with saying, "Though we currently do not know how to prove the existence of the soul, in the future we will"?
27. Give an example of a true statement with no empirical meaning.
28. What is falsifiability, and why is it important to empirical meaning? Give examples.
29. How can an attitude statement be transformed into an empirical one?

30. What is a weasel word, and what effect does it have when it occurs in a statement?
31. Show how a statement (the same one) can be used in different ways to be either empirical, analytic, attitude, or metaphysical.
32. Five types of statements are discussed in this chapter. Which of them are empirically meaningful, and which of them are empirically meaningless?
33. How might you try to convince a person that a statement is empirically meaningless?
34. Give an example of an important human experience that is not empirical.

❏ Chapter Exercises

I.

Based on your reading of this chapter, decide whether each of the following statements is empirical, analytic, value, attitude, or metaphysical. Consider how each statement is usually used or is most likely to be used. Explain your answers. Suggested answers are provided in the back of the book for the items marked with an asterisk.

A. (Fairly Easy)

1. Bigfoot exists.*
2. Down with apartheid!*
3. A hat is something you wear on your head.*
4. The number of elephants in Africa has fallen below 20,000.*
5. My grandmother is in heaven.*
6. Late students have to crash classes.
7. Red is a color.
8. Marilyn died of cancer.
9. Oliver North did the right thing when he lied to Congress.
10. Force = mass × acceleration (physics textbook).
11. The sun is mostly hydrogen.
12. Flies are insects.
13. Race-car drivers are the most loathsome bunch of people you could ever hope to meet.
14. Picasso was the best painter of the 20th century.

15. Saint Michael drove the ghosts out of our house (statement by Janet Smurl to UPI, 1986).
16. Cacti can grow and survive indefinitely on the moon without any special attention from a gardener.
17. Little green men live on Mars.
18. God is the supreme being.
19. You can't trust communists.
20. Many people have been abducted by aliens from outer space.

B. *(Moderately Difficult)*

21. All humans are born equal.*
22. God created Himself.*
23. Abortion is wrong.*
24. People cannot prove that they exist.
25. Every kid on this block is the toughest kid on this block.
26. A copy can never be as good as the original.
27. All time is happening at the same time (statement by Shirley MacLaine in the *Los Angeles Times,* July 20, 1987).

II.

Based on your reading of this chapter, decide whether each of the following statements has empirical meaning. Again, consider how each statement is usually used or is most likely to be used. Explain your answers. Suggested answers are provided in the back of the book for the items marked with an asterisk.

1. Unicorns do not exist.*
2. Computers actually think.*
3. All prayers are answered.*
4. Plants and trees know when it's winter.
5. People always do what they want to do.
6. The mysterious disappearances in the Bermuda Triangle are caused by a time warp.
7. We can't be certain of anything.
8. My pet rock is in pain.
9. Rudy has a sprained ankle, and he's in pain.
10. The purpose of life is to have pleasure.
11. Everything I experience is actually just a dream.
12. Nothing happens before its time.

13. The Jones house is haunted.
14. There are no coincidences; there is a reason for everything that happens.
15. Nobody's perfect.

III.

Read each of the following items. Then, based on that information, identify the statement in quotes as empirical, analytic, value, attitude, metaphysical, or none of the above. In the back of the book you will find suggested answers to the items marked with an asterisk.

1. Every act is selfish. Even if you give up your life for another person, you are ultimately doing it for yourself, because you wouldn't do it otherwise. (Identify: "Every act is selfish.") *
2. The recent explosion of interest in the occult is a good thing, because it provides people with an exciting pastime. (Identify: "The recent explosion of interest in the occult is a good thing.") *
3. Nothing ever dies. Science tells us that. Nothing ever dies, it just changes form (statement by Shirley MacLaine on the *Donahue* show, September 9, 1985). (Identify: "Nothing ever dies.") *
4. All human beings are mortal. They have to be. If they weren't, they wouldn't be human beings. (Identify: "All human beings are mortal.")
5. The universe is only 6,000 years old. It was created with simply the appearance of being much older. Fossilized dinosaur bones, the geological column, continental drift, the starlight that seems to require millions of years to arrive at earth—all these are just part of the illusion that the universe is billions of years old. (Identify: "The universe is only 6,000 years old.")
6. My neighbor, Jane, is a genuine psychic, but she can't be tested in the laboratory. In fact, she can't be tested anywhere, because psychic phenomena are not things that can be proven. (Identify: "Jane is a genuine psychic.")
7. My son is 35, and he still hasn't found a career. This worries me, because he's not getting any younger. (Identify: "He's not getting any younger.")
8. Jeff is a psychic, because he can read my mind. Whenever we're within 10 feet of each other, he always knows what I'm thinking. (Identify: "He can read my mind.")

CHAPTER 3

❏ ❏ ❏ ❏ ❏ ❏ ❏

Common Fallacies

Arguments, like men, are often pretenders.

Plato

In the previous chapter we analyzed individual statements for their meaning. In the present chapter we will look at statements in groups, called arguments. Whereas the point to giving our attention to language is to avoid illusions about what we are saying in any particular statement, the point to studying arguments is to recognize when one statement is not given adequate support from other statements, creating a fallacy. In both cases our primary objective is to learn to spot errors in reasoning about New Age ideas.

Before we begin our discussion of fallacious arguments, we should say a few words about what an argument is and practice identifying one.

❏ What Is an Argument?

The word *argument* in everyday speech means a dispute between two or more people who disagree on something. We might, for example, get into an argument over who is to pay the bill at a restaurant or over whether abortion is right or wrong. But in the study of logic or critical thinking the word *argument* means something quite different. It stands for the basic unit of reasoning in which an assertion is derived from one or more other assertions. Someone makes an argument when he or she makes a claim (conclusion) and gives one or more reasons (premises) in support of it. For example:

Robert: Henrietta's car is in her driveway, so she's at home now.

In this act of reasoning Robert is drawing a conclusion (Henrietta is at home now) from a premise (Henrietta's car is in her driveway). If we diagram this argument, it looks like this:

Premise: Henrietta's car is in the driveway.
_____
Conclusion: Therefore, Henrietta is at home now.

And here's a more complicated example:

Joy: Fred is registered, because if he's enrolled, then he's registered, and he is enrolled.

Joy derives (or infers) that Fred is registered from the fact that he is enrolled and the fact that in order to be enrolled, he has to be registered. Her argument can be diagrammed as follows:

Premises: 1. If Fred is enrolled, he's registered.
              2. Fred is enrolled.
_____
Conclusion: Therefore, Fred is registered.

This process of diagramming is just a handy way of clarifying the structure of any argument. By listing the premise(s) first, drawing a line, and then giving the conclusion, we make it quite obvious what's what in the argument.

Premise and Conclusion Indicators

Notice in Robert's argument that the word *so* signals the coming of the conclusion. Several other words are also commonly used to do this job. For example, Robert could have indicated his conclusion by using the word *therefore* instead. Notice, too, that Joy uses the word *because* to indicate her premises.

Here is a handy list of terms that are commonly used to announce the coming of one or more premises:

Premise Indicators
1. because
2. for
3. as
4. for the reason that
5. from the fact that
6. can be inferred from

And here's a handy list of terms that often signal the coming of a conclusion:

Conclusion Indicators
1. hence
2. thus
3. therefore
4. consequently
5. it follows that
6. the result is that
7. the point is that

These verbal clues are very helpful, but we need to be aware that they're not always present. Sometimes we have only the context to determine whether a statement is a conclusion or a premise.

The Organization of an Argument

The process of figuring out exactly what a person's argument is (if indeed he or she has one) can be difficult and tedious. In everyday speech the conclusion and premise(s) of an argument occur in no particular order. In Robert's argument, for example, the conclusion comes at the end. In Joy's argument, on the other hand, the conclusion comes at the beginning. Sometimes, the conclusion occurs in the middle of a long-winded paragraph. Sometimes the conclusion is not even mentioned, and you, the listener, are expected to fill it in. To get a clear picture of the argument, we need to identify which statement is the conclusion and which statement(s) is (are) the premise(s). The exercise "Arguments" at the end of the chapter will provide practice in doing this. It would be a good idea to complete this exercise before beginning the next section.

❑ What Is a Fallacy?

Normally, when we speak of a fallacy, we mean a notion that's false. Thus, the idea that chocolate causes acne and the notion that a rabbit's foot guarantees good luck are fallacies in this sense. When I use the word *fallacy* in this book, however, I mean a defective argument, one in which the premises do not provide an adequate basis for the conclusion.

The common fallacies are patterns of bad reasoning that we encounter practically every day when reading a newspaper article, listening to a commentator on radio or television, or talking with friends. No one is immune to them: we are all, from time to time, taken in by them or commit them ourselves. Naturally, they pop up in discussions about the paranormal, but they can occur anytime, regardless of the subject we are dealing with. The best way to ensure against them is to become aware of them and develop the ability to spot them when they occur.

In this chapter we will learn to recognize 16 of the common fallacies as they occur when people are talking and reasoning about paranormal issues. The fallacies we'll examine are:

1. ad Hominem (Attack the Person)
2. Genetic
3. Appeal to Ignorance
4. Appeal to Authority
5. Two Wrongs Make a Right
6. Bandwagon
7. Past Practice
8. Begging the Question
9. Irrelevant Thesis
10. Equivocation
11. False Cause
12. Poisoning the Well
13. False Dichotomy
14. Loaded Question
15. Hasty Generalization
16. Straw Man

In the next chapter we will encounter a different group of fallacies: ones that seem peculiar to the topic of the paranormal. In all, 30 fallacies will be covered in this book, but we should not think of them as a complete list. Some logic books describe over 100 fallacies, and even they do not pretend to be exhaustive. It seems unlikely that there could ever be a complete list of the errors we can make when reasoning.

Ad Hominem

The traditional Latin term for the first fallacy is *argumentum ad hominem,* and it means, literally, "argument against the man." In ordinary English it should be translated "attack the person." It occurs when someone attempts to refute a person's claim by attacking that person rather than the claim. The basic structure of the ad Hominem Fallacy looks like this:

> There is something objectionable about so and so.
> _____
> Therefore, so and so's claim is false.

It is a fallacy because the person's character has no bearing on the truth or falsity of the claim. No matter how rotten a person's character may be, his or her assertion may still be true. In this argument:

> James Randi says that Peter Popoff is a charlatan. But only a fool would listen to Randi, because he's an atheist.

(paraphrased from a comment by a member of the audience on the *Sally Jessy Raphael* TV interview show) the speaker tries to refute Randi's claim by attacking him personally. The argument fails from a logical point of view, because even if Randi is an atheist, Popoff may still be a charlatan. Whether Popoff is actually a charlatan can be determined only by objective observation of the evidence, not by checking on Randi's religious orientation.

Here are two more examples:

> Professor Jones maintains that some people have ESP. That's absurd! Do you realize he's a communist?

> According to Derrin, the idea that ships and airplanes mysteriously disappear in the Bermuda Triangle is just a hoax. Well, I don't believe Derrin, because he's a radical.

In these examples the speakers, instead of citing evidence that discredits the claim, merely resort to personal slander.

Of course, it is not always totally irrelevant to make reference to a person's character in order to refute what she says. In a court of law, for example, to point out that a certain witness is known to be a chronic liar is to show good reason to doubt his testimony. I hasten to add, however, that a reason for doubting a piece of testimony is not proof that it is false. The truth or falsity of a claim depends ultimately on the facts, not on who makes it.

Genetic

The Genetic Fallacy occurs when a person argues that a claim is false because of how it originated. The basic structure looks like this:

We can explain why so and so asserts that A is true.

Therefore, A is false.

This argument is fallacious because the causal factors that explain how a claim arose are irrelevant to determining whether the claim is true or false. Here are three examples of this fallacy:

> Thornton tells us that wearing quartz crystals around our neck will not cure our respiratory problems. But what do you expect him to say? He's a very skeptical person.

> Elizabeth consults her Ouija board every night before she goes to bed, and she says it has never been wrong. What nonsense! She believes this only because she was steeped in the occult from the time she was a baby.

> The Lutz family contends that its house in Amityville is haunted. I would, too, if I could make a $10-million movie from it!

In each case the only reason offered as evidence against the claim is an (irrelevant) account of how it arose: Thornton says what he says only because he's a skeptic; Elizabeth says what she says only because she's a believer; and the Lutz family says what it says only because it wants to make money. But even if Thornton has the bias of a skeptic, he could still be right about crystals. And even if Elizabeth was saturated in the occult from infancy, she could still be right about her Ouija board. And even if the Lutz family is trying to make money, this fact does not prove that its house is not haunted.

All of the evidence offered in these examples is irrelevant to determining whether the claims are true. If we want to find out whether crystals really cure respiratory problems, for example, we'll have to carefully observe people who wear them (and people who don't!). (See the section in Chapter 5 on controlled studies.) If we want to find out if Elizabeth's Ouija board is really truthful, we'll have to observe and record what it says and faithfully check to see if the pronouncements are correct. And if we want to find out whether there are inexplicable and spooky goings-on at the Lutz house, we will have to go there and observe them ourselves, being careful to eliminate mundane causes.

Whether a person's claim is true or false depends solely on whether strong evidence can be marshaled in support of it. And this question of evidence must be sharply distinguished from any other factors that explain why a person makes the claim.

Appeal to Ignorance

The Fallacy of Appeal to Ignorance (Latin: *argumentum ad ignorantium*) can be committed in one of two ways. The first way is to draw the conclusion that an idea is false because it has never been proved true, and the second way is to draw the conclusion that an idea is true because it has never been proved false. The basic form of this reasoning looks like this:

> P has never been proved true.
> _____
>
> Therefore, P is false.

or: P has never been proved false.
>   _____
>
>   Therefore, P is true.

This is a fallacy because the fact that something has not been proved true does not make it false, and vice versa. Here are some examples:

> They have never been able to come up with concrete evidence that bigfoot exists; thus, we can be sure that this creature does not exist.

> Ghosts must exist at the Smurl house in West Pittston, because skeptics have never proved that they don't.

> ESP must not be real, because scientific testing has never come up with a shred of solid evidence for it.

> Why, of course there's life after death. Do you know of any proof that there isn't?

In all of these examples an attempt is made to establish the truth of a proposition by a lack of proof to the contrary. But a lack of proof is not a proof; this is attempting to get something from nothing.

A lack of proof proves nothing at all, except that we are ignorant. It's true that we have no compelling evidence for bigfoot, but perhaps tomorrow we'll get it! The fact that no one has proved that there are no ghosts in the Smurl house does not mean that there are ghosts there. (Incidently, how would we go about showing that a ghost was not present at a given location? The concept of a ghost is a metaphysical one, not an empirical one. At best, it is extremely unclear what would count as evidence for or against the presence of ghosts.) It's also true that no solid evidence for ESP has ever been found, but how can we be sure that we tested the right people in the right circumstances? Again, it's always possible that tomorrow we may find a person who actually has ESP. And it's true that we have no proof that life after death does not exist, but this is not evidence that life after death does exist.

A word of caution is in order here. Sometimes an appeal to a lack of evidence is not fallacious. If, for example, after examining a urine specimen a doctor says that there is no blood in it, the claim is justified. The argument would look like this:

> There is [after careful examination] no evidence of blood in your urine; therefore, you do not have blood in your urine.

This is a good argument. The difference here is that an investigation has been undertaken that should reveal blood in the urine if it was actually there. In the four previous examples, on the other hand, no investigation (if such was possible) was mentioned.

In our law courts a person is presumed innocent until proved guilty. It might seem that we should have to call this an example of the Fallacy of Appeal to Ignorance, but this is not so. The courts do not maintain that a lack of proof of guilt is a proof of innocence. They maintain only that until proof of guilt is shown, innocence should be presumed.

Appeal to Authority

We frequently refer to authorities when we wish to strengthen our position in a dispute. There is nothing wrong with doing this as long as the person referred to is really an authority on the subject at issue. When he or she isn't, the Fallacy of Appeal to Authority (Latin: *ad verecundiam*) is committed. The basic structure of this fallacy looks like this:

> So and so says that A is true [said when so and so is not an authority].
> _____
> Therefore, A is true.

Here's an example of this fallacy:

> Chocolate causes cancer. There can be no doubt about this, because Robert Smith said so, and he is an admiral in the navy.

In this case the fallacy is committed because Robert Smith is (probably) not a cancer researcher. However, if it turns out that he is an expert on this subject, then no fallacy is committed. Of course, you may not know whether the fallacy is committed unless you know that the person referred to is not an authority, and this may take some investigating.

In a deeper sense every appeal to authority is a fallacy, because only facts, not testimony, constitute proof. The only good reason to appeal to a genuine authority is that the person knows the important facts. Hence, a stronger way to argue, and the best way of avoiding the Appeal to Authority Fallacy, is to cite facts instead of testimony.

Attempts are often made to validate New Age ideas by referring to authorities. Here we must be especially alert to the Appeal to Authority Fallacy, because when a phenomenon is unproved, so-called authorities are unproved as well. Let's examine the following argument:

> Channeling is real, because Shirley MacLaine talks about her numerous experiences with channeling in her book.

(Channeling is the New Age form of mediumship. A person's spirit supposedly leaves the body, and another spirit—usually from a dead person—enters the body and speaks through it.)

Is MacLaine an expert on channeling? Is *anyone* an expert on channeling? How can we determine who is and who is not an expert on this subject? If it were a subject like snakes, asteroids, mountain climbing, or jet propulsion, there would be no problem in deciding who the experts were. Why is this? The answer is that snakes, asteroids, mountain climbing, and jet propulsion are clearly empirical phenomena. This makes it possible to check on any claim that a supposed expert might make about them. And we can do this checking, even if we're not experts. With channeling, on the other hand, it's different. Channeling is a metaphysical concept (involving the notion of the soul), and this means that we do not have the usual methods of checking and verifying. Compare the following two claims made by people supposed to be experts:

> Expert on snakes: Coral snakes are poisonous.

> "Expert" on channeling: Ms. Loren channels a 10-million-year-old spirit being from the seventh dimension, named Zune.

Now, it would be easy to check out the snake expert's claim: we simply arrange for a coral snake to bite a rat and watch what happens. But how could we check out the channeling expert's claim? What would prove that he's really an expert? We simply do not know what to look for that would verify his claim; consequently, we cannot declare him an expert on channeling.

There can, however, be experts (authorities) on the behavior of channelers, and there can be experts on the literature written about channeling. This is because claims made about these topics are empirically meaningful and can be verified by observations.

Now let's look at another example:

> Father McKinna was at the Smurls' house, and he says there are ghosts there. Therefore there were ghosts there [Ed Warren, a demonologist, on the *Sally Jessy Raphael* show, 1987].

Is Father McKinna an expert on ghosts? Again we can ask: Is anyone an expert on ghosts? How could we tell an expert from a nonexpert? We simply have no reliable way of bestowing this honor on a person, because we're dealing with a metaphysical concept. If the term *ghost* had an empirical definition, we could check on Father McKinna's testimony, but without this, we cannot validate his authority. Warren, therefore, is committing the Fallacy of Appeal to Authority.

Two Wrongs Make a Right

The Fallacy of Two Wrongs Make a Right is committed when we try to justify what we did by accusing someone else of doing the same thing. The Latin *tu ouoque* is the traditional name for this one, and it means "you also," or (as we would say) "look who's talking." The basic form looks like this:

> But you do it too [or someone else does].
>
> Therefore, it's all right if I do it.

Here's an example:

> Who are you to judge my drinking? I've seen you down two six-packs while watching the ball game!

This method of arguing can be very effective in diffusing an attack, and this is undoubtedly why it is so frequently used. The attackers are (at least momentarily) disarmed with the feeling that they have no right to make the accusation, because they are just as guilty. The guilt of the accusers, however, is irrelevant to the question of the guilt or innocence of the accused, and it cannot be used as a defense. Look at this example from the *Sally Jessy Raphael* show (1987):

Henry Gordon: When I see a book being published, I become immediately suspicious [that the story is a hoax].

Ed Warren: But you've got a book published too, haven't you?

Gordon accuses Warren of having published a fictional ghost story as factual merely for profit, and Warren reacts defensively. He hopes to divert some of the heat by accusing Gordon of also having published a book for profit. At best, Warren's maneuver establishes the guilt of his accuser; it does not demonstrate his own innocence. (In any case, the sharp observer will note that the issue of profit from a story is separate from the issue of evidence for a story. Hence, Warren's fallacious argument is also a method of getting off the track.)

Let's look at another example. Imagine that Mary, who has been injured by advice from people calling themselves psychics, is trying to prevent the same thing from happening to Bess:

Mary: If you give your trust and your money to a psychic, you're making a big mistake.

Bess: Who are you to talk? You've been visiting psychics for 10 years!

Bess may find it comforting to know that her friend has been visiting psychics, but this does not justify her decision to do the same.

Bandwagon

We commit the Bandwagon Fallacy when we conclude that an idea is true because a lot of people believe it or that a certain practice is right because a lot of people do it. The Latin term is *argumentum ad populum,* which means "appeal to the people." (Other translations are "appeal to the gallery," "appeal to the masses," and "appeal to the mob.") The basic form is:

Lots of people do X.

Therefore, it's all right to do X.

or: Lots of people believe that A is true.

Therefore, A is true.

The fact that many people do something does not necessarily make it right, and general assent to a claim does not prove it to be true. The popularity of this fallacy attests to the influence of society on our thinking. Being logical often requires an awareness of social pressure and an ability to reject it. Let's look at some examples:

> Everybody believes that the earth is flat [said in the ninth century]. Therefore, the earth is flat.

> Of course it's all right to go to Dr. Penross to get his colored-light treatment for my cancer. Practically everyone with cancer in my town goes to him for this treatment.

> Astrology couldn't be baloney. Too many people believe in it.

In the ninth century the earth was round even though nearly everyone believed that it was flat. Facts tend to be rather stubborn that way. And the fact that many or all cancer patients in your town seek the services of a certain (questionable) doctor doesn't mean that it would be wise for you to do so. The time you waste on a quack could be fatal. As for astrology, whether it works can be established only by making systematic observations, not by counting the number of people who believe in it.

Past Practice

The Fallacy of Past Practice is a variation of the Bandwagon Fallacy. The form is:

> We have been doing this for a long time.
> ———————————————————
> Therefore, we should continue to do it.

The appeal to tradition seems to make good sense, because we learn a great deal from the past experiences of others. At the same time, it is a mistake to think that just because something has been practiced for a long time, it must be right. For example:

> Why, of course slavery is right and proper. After all, it's been a solid American tradition for over 100 years [said by an antebellum plantation owner].

Before any appeal to tradition is accepted, there are two points to bear in mind: (1) Traditions, even very long ones, can be unwise or morally wrong. (2) A tradition, even if it was not wrong before, may need to be changed or discarded because of changing circumstances.

Now let's look at two examples from the paranormal:

For many years our family has been going to visit Ruby Cummins [a medium], and she has enabled my mother, my father, and me to communicate with my dead brother. Therefore, we should not give up this valuable tradition.

Astrology has been around for centuries, and lots of people still use it. So why should they stop now?

It may be difficult to break with family tradition, but sometimes doing so is indicated by new knowledge. If Cummins is exposed as a charlatan who uses magician's techniques to create the illusion of spirits in her seances, tradition becomes a feeble reason to continue seeking her services. (Though, from a psychological point of view, it's not difficult to understand why a person or a family might wish to do so.) And astrology is indeed very old; it dates back to at least the second century B.C., but modern science has rejected it because it is useless as a tool for making predictions (Steiner, 1989). As a form of entertainment astrology can be fun, but basing important decisions on it may have unfortunate results that could have been averted by critical thinking.

Begging the Question

The Fallacy of Begging the Question (Latin: *petitio principii*) occurs when our conclusion is contained in (or assumed by) our premise(s). Another term for this way of arguing is circular reasoning, and its basic structure looks like this:

A is true because A is true.

or: A is true because B is true, and
B is true because A is true.

or: A is true because B is true, and
B is true because C is true, and
C is true because A is true.

By extension we can see that a circular argument can be of any length, but the essential characteristic in all variations is that they end up where they started. Two examples having the first form are:

Kelly: How do you know that Heather can levitate?

Sarah: Because she can lift her whole body off the ground just by thinking about it.

Bob: What makes you think you saw a real ghost?

Joe: Because I saw it.

The statement "Heather can levitate" is saying essentially the same thing as "Heather can lift her whole body off the ground just by thinking about it." Thus, the latter does not offer a reason in support of the former; it merely restates it. Similarly, Joe does not offer a reason for asserting that what he saw was real; he merely repeats his original assertion that he saw a real ghost.

Here's a subtler example having the first form:

We know that bigfoot exists, because we have its footprints in the forests of southern Oregon.

This is reasoning in a circle because the conclusion (bigfoot exists) must be accepted before the premise (bigfoot made the Oregon footprints) is accepted. The argument proves nothing, because the premise contains (assumes) the conclusion. Hence, the premise does not support the conclusion, it merely repeats it.

Now here's an example of the Fallacy of Begging the Question having the second form:

Trevor: Many people employ dowsers, because dowsing really works. [Dowsing is the process of walking over the land while holding a stick in order to locate underground water sources.]

Spencer: How do you know that dowsing really works?

Trevor: Because lots of people use dowsers.

Trevor supports his assertion that many people employ dowsers by saying that dowsing works. But then Trevor's reason for saying that dowsing works is that many people employ dowsers. This brings us full circle, and the net value of such an argument is zero, because it ultimately fails to provide a reason (premise) for the conclusion.

Irrelevant Thesis

The Fallacy of Irrelevant Thesis (Latin: *ignoratio elenchi*) takes place when someone tries to support a conclusion by offering reasons that actually have no bearing on the issue in question. The basic form is:

A is true [when A is irrelevant to the truth of B].

Therefore, B is true.

For example:

> *Son:* Do you think I'm too young to get married?
>
> *Father:* No, son. Marriage is a perfectly natural thing.

The father is not addressing the issue at hand: is it too early for the son to get married? Saying that marriage is natural does not tell the son at what age he should get married. If the irrelevance of the father's premise goes unnoticed, the son just may take his father's argument as a strong reason to get married now.

Let's look at another case: On the *Sally Jessy Raphael* show (mentioned above) Warren offered a videotape as evidence to prove his claim about ghosts in the Smurls' house. Warren said the tape showed the exorcism of demons from a man's body. (But strictly speaking, all we could see was a man sitting slumped in a chair and drooling onto his shirt.) Warren's argument looks like this:

A certain farmer is possessed by demons.

Therefore, the Smurls' house is haunted.

Warren's tape was very unconvincing, but even if it did show demons being exorcised (whatever that means) from a person's body, this would not prove there were ghosts in the Smurls' house. The farmer lived in a different state and had no connection with the Smurls at all.

Now listen to the irrelevancy in the following:

> *Tilly:* Oh, yes, UFOs are real; we're being visited by beings from another world.
>
> *Jason:* What makes you think so?
>
> *Tilly:* Well, they've discovered a lot of things lately that they used to think weren't true. For example, frogs cause warts, and continents actually move.

Tilly's premise is quite irrelevant to her conclusion. The movement of continents and warts caused by frogs have no bearing on the question of whether UFOs are real.

Notice that many fallacies we have discussed involve premises that are irrelevant to the conclusion (for example, the ad Hominem and Genetic fallacies). Therefore, a fallacy should be called an Irrelevant Thesis only if some other fallacy name does not apply.

Equivocation

Most words have more than one meaning. This fact makes it possible to create fallacious arguments, because a key term is used in one sense in a premise and in another sense in the conclusion. The basic form is:

Premise: [statement(s) using term X in sense 1]

Conclusion: [statement using term X in sense 2]

We can illustrate this fallacy by the following humorous example:

The average family has 2.5 children, and John's family is very average. So, John's family must have 2.5 children.

In the conclusion the term *average* means a mathematical figure (2.5). In one of the two premises, the term *average* means "normal," or "ordinary." The Equivocation Fallacy is being committed because the inference turns on the ambiguity in meaning of this word. Now let's look at an example provided by one of my students:

What's wrong with taking LSD? It's just a chemical, and the bloodstream is full of chemicals all the time anyway.

This argument turns on the double meaning of *chemical*. The two different senses (meanings) used are:

1. a synthetically produced substance; a drug
2. a naturally produced substance; a hormone

Here is another example:

Love is the principle of attraction that holds the universe together. It keeps electrons in orbit around the nucleus. It keeps the planets in orbit around the sun. It is what holds all matter together, from the smallest atom to the largest galaxy. Hence, we can see that when two people fall in love, they are obeying a universal law of nature.

In this argument the word *love* is used in the premise to mean the physical force that draws two pieces of matter together, and in the conclusion the word *love* means the feeling of attachment or affection between two people. Since these are very different sorts of things, it is fallacious to think that we are speaking of the same thing in the conclusion as we are in the premise.

False Cause

The Latin name for the Fallacy of False Cause is *post hoc, ergo propter hoc,* which means "after this, therefore because of this." The Latin is often abbreviated *post hoc.* We commit this fallacy when we infer a causal connection between two succeeding events when no such connection has been established. The structure of this argument looks like this:

> After A happens, B happens.
> ———————————————
> Therefore, A causes B.

Several years ago, *Life* magazine reported that a man had cured his cancer by eating a strict diet of grain foods for six months. But the mere fact that one event follows another event in time is not enough to prove that the two events are causally related. When one event follows another with regularity, the two are said to be correlated. But correlation is not the same as causation. Although it is true that the man's cancer disappeared after the grain diet, this is not proof that the diet cured the cancer. Any number of other factors could account for the cure.

Here are two more examples of this fallacy:

> I don't use birth control pills or any contraceptive gadgets, because I've got a better way. I have found I can keep from getting pregnant by simply telling myself, silently before sex, that I won't. It's the power of mind over matter. I've been doing this for two years, and I haven't gotten pregnant. I'm really excited about this discovery. It's a completely safe and effective method of birth control.

> I know a woman who had been troubled with arthritis for 20 years. Then one time she went to see Oral Roberts at one of his faith-healing crusades. Ever since then she's been just great. Obviously, she was cured by that visit to Oral Roberts [woman in the audience on the *Sally Jessy Raphael* show, 1985].

Correlation does suggest a possible causal relationship, but by itself it is not proof. The fact that the woman did not get pregnant could be explained by any number of things, such as that she (or her mate) might have been sterile. The recovery from arthritis could have been just a coincidence. In order to rule out these possibilities a controlled study would have to be done. We will examine this procedure in Chapter 5.

Poisoning the Well

The Fallacy of Poisoning the Well occurs when we attempt to put our opponents in a position that makes it impossible for them to contest our position. It is a fallacious tactic because it closes the door on the important process of critical review. The basic form looks like this:

> You are in position X.
> _____
> Therefore, everything you say against my position is invalid.

The name of this fallacy conveys the idea that once a well has been poisoned, all samples of water taken from it will be polluted. Here's an example of this fallacy:

> *Ron:* Before we debate this issue [of the validity of the Ouija board], let me ask you, do you believe that spirits exist?
>
> *Linda:* No, I don't.
>
> *Ron:* In that case you are not qualified to debate this issue.

Ron is poisoning the well, because he is discrediting anything that Linda might have to say about the Ouija board even before she says it. He is rejecting her argumentation without having heard it.

Here's another example:

> Beware of those who question my psychic power, for their minds are closed to the truth.

This is a ploy often used by charlatans to fortify their audience against skeptics. It is an insidious attempt to inhibit critical thinking.

In the following example, Paula poisons the well for all men:

> *Paula:* I believe there is something called feminine intuition, and I don't even want to listen to Hank. He's a man, and men can't possibly know anything about it.

How can Paula know what Hank has to say before she hears it? Could her feminine intuition be leading her astray?

False Dichotomy

The Fallacy of False Dichotomy is committed when only two options are stated and others are overlooked. The basic form is:

    1. Either A or B is true.   [when A and B are not the only two
    2. A is not true.   possibilities]

    Therefore, B is true.

or: 1. Either A or B is true.   [when A and B are not the only two
    2. B is not true.   possibilities]

    Therefore, A is true.

For example:

> Either John wants to learn astrology or he wants to continue bungling through life as he has been. Now, I'm sure he doesn't want to continue bungling through life, so he'll be glad to learn astrology.

The first premise in this argument assumes what is false: that John is stuck with just these two options. The argument can be refuted (and the fallacy exposed) by showing that both options can be avoided or that some third option is available. After all, John might not learn astrology *and* might avoid bungling through life. Or he might recognize and select a third option: professional help through counseling.

Now let's listen to one of my students committing this fallacy:

> Either I was hallucinating or I actually saw Uri Geller bend that spoon with his mind. Now, I know I wasn't hallucinating (because other people saw it, too), so Geller actually did bend that spoon with his mind.

The two possibilities offered here are certainly not the only ones. A third possibility is that Geller is a skilled magician using sleight-of-hand to create illusions.

Here is a third example of this fallacy:

> Either scientists can explain the strange objects seen in the sky over Gulf Breeze, Florida, or these objects are piloted by visitors from outer space. Scientists cannot explain these objects, so they must be visitors from outer space.

This reasoning actually leads many people to believe that we are being watched by extraterrestrials. But we can find serious fault with this reasoning even without denying the possibility of visitors from outer space. With a little reflection we can realize that it is quite possible that the unexplained images have ordinary causes that scientific investigators have failed to discover. In other words, if we think a little bit deeper, we can realize that the dichotomy in the first premise of this argument is false.

Loaded Question

A loaded question is one that embodies a questionable assumption, and if we answer the question we indicate agreement with that assumption. Thus, we can say that any argument containing a loaded question is fallacious. For example, if a man answers this question:

Have you stopped beating your wife yet?

he is falling into a trap of self-condemnation. The question beckons for a simple yes or no. But if the man answers yes, it implies that he has beaten his wife. If he answers no, it implies that he is still beating his wife. So, no matter which way he answers, he appears guilty. Obviously, the way to deal with this question is to expose and reject the questionable assumption: that he is a wife beater.

Now let's look at another example:

Are you going to continue leaving your life to chance? [This appeared in an advertisement for a psychic palm reader.]

The palm reader's objectionable assumption here is that the people addressed have been leaving their life to chance, and the implied conclusion is that they should use her services. But they should question this assumption before they make any attempt to answer her inquiry. It's important for them to remember that they can always question the question: "Have I *really* been leaving my life to chance?" "Would the guidance of a psychic palm reader *really* eliminate the element of chance from my life?"

Spotting the underlying assumption is the only way of avoiding the trap. In this example:

Are you still wasting your time and money on school? [Ingrid, who left school to join a cult of channelers in Oregon, is speaking to Tracy, who was her roommate in college.]

Tracy can avert the feeling that this question deserves an answer if she recognizes and rejects the supposition that time and money spent on school are wasted.

Here's another example that might catch us off guard:

Why have extraterrestrials come to our planet?

This question invites us immediately to speculate about the motives of space aliens. It assumes that contact with extraterrestrials is an established fact, which it isn't. Realizing that this is a questionable assumption, we can simply reject the question and turn to more fruitful ones, such as "Do we have strong evidence of visitations by extraterrestrials?"

Hasty Generalization

We commit the Fallacy of Hasty Generalization when we draw a conclusion about an entire class of things or people from just a few observed cases. The basic pattern is:

A few *X*s have quality *m*.
_____
Therefore, all *X*s have quality *m*.

This is a fallacious way to argue because the sample is too small to warrant the general conclusion. Here are some examples:

California women believe in astrology. I know, because I've dated four women from California, and all of them were into astrology.

The five faith healers we've investigated have turned out to be flimflam artists. From this evidence we can safely conclude that all faith healers are flimflam artists.

Every scientist I've talked to seemed closed minded on this subject [reincarnation]. Thus, it seems you're wasting your time if you try to talk to any scientist about it.

The man who concludes that all women from California believe in astrology because four of them do is making a hasty generalization. The fact that five faith healers are charlatans is thin support for the sweeping conclusion that all are. And though it may be true that some scientists are closed minded about reincarnation, this does not mean that all are.

It is easy to find the source of this fallacy. It stems from our natural ability to learn from our experiences. As children we quickly learned that a flame is hot by touching it. We didn't have to repeat the experience too many times to realize that all flames are hot. Thus, our tendency to generalize from our experiences has obvious survival value. But at the same time, we need to be on guard to make sure that it does not deceive us.

Straw Man

The Straw Man Fallacy occurs when one person misrepresents the view of another person in order to make him or her an easy target. The procedure is to create a misdescription of someone's position and then to attack this false picture with the hope of refuting the actual position. This is a common tactic of politicians and others who want to quickly demolish their opponents. The basic idea is:

> My opponent's position is A, and A has serious faults [when A is not the opponent's position].
> _____
> Therefore, my opponent's position should be rejected.

The flaws in A may be real, but they are irrelevant, because A is not the opponent's position. The arguer succeeds, if at all, in knocking down a straw man instead of the real man. Here's an example:

> *Megan:* Judith says she doubts that UFOs come from outer space. But I don't understand how she can close her mind to the possibility of intelligent life in other parts of the universe.

Did Judith say that her mind was closed to the possibility of extraterrestrial life? No, she merely said that she doubted that UFOs were visitors from outer space. That's different, because unidentified flying objects might be anything from clouds to space aliens. Megan is not actually attacking Judith's position at all.

Another example is:

> *Penn:* Scientists don't take psychic phenomena seriously, because they refuse to consider anything that they don't understand.

Is Penn accurately representing the position of scientists? Would scientists agree with his description of them? Obviously not, because many scientists today are working to understand what they don't, now, understand. For example, some researchers are working hard to find the cause of Alzheimer's disease, and others are trying to understand the braided rings of Saturn. Penn, instead of attacking scientists, is merely attacking a caricature of them. His attack, therefore, is fallacious.

❏ **Chapter Review Questions**

1. What is an argument, as it is defined in this chapter?
2. What are the names of the two parts of an argument?
3. Before looking them up, name as many premise indicators as you can.
4. Before looking them up, name as many conclusion indicators as you can.
5. What is a fallacy, as it is defined in this chapter?
6. What is the ad Hominem Fallacy? Why is it a fallacy? Write the structure, and make up an example.
7. What is the Genetic Fallacy? Why is it a fallacy? Write the structure, and make up an example.
8. What is the Fallacy of Appeal to Ignorance? Why is it a fallacy? Write the structure, and make up an example.
9. What is the Fallacy of Appeal to Authority? Why is it a fallacy? Write the structure, and make up an example.
10. What is the Fallacy of Two Wrongs? Why is it a fallacy? Write the structure, and make up an example.
11. What is the Fallacy of the Bandwagon? Why is it a fallacy? Write the structure, and make up an example.
12. What is the Past Practice Fallacy? Why is it a fallacy? Write the structure, and make up an example.
13. What is the Fallacy of Begging the Question? Why is it a fallacy? Write the structure, and make up an example.
14. What is the Fallacy of Irrelevant Thesis? Why is it a fallacy? Write the structure, and make up an example.
15. What is the Fallacy of Equivocation? Why is it a fallacy? Write the structure, and make up an example.
16. What is the False Cause Fallacy? Why is it a fallacy? Write the structure, and make up an example.
17. What is the Fallacy of Poisoning the Well? Why is it a fallacy? Write the structure, and make up an example.
18. What is the Fallacy of False Dichotomy? Why is it a fallacy? Write the structure, and make up an example.
19. What is the Loaded Question Fallacy? Why is it a fallacy? Make up an example.
20. What is the Fallacy of Hasty Generalization? Why is it a fallacy? Write the structure, and make up an example.

21. What is the Straw Man Fallacy? Why is it a fallacy? Write the structure, and make up an example.

❏ Chapter Exercises

I. Arguments

Look over the following items, and determine which of them are arguments and which are not. Diagram those that are arguments to show the conclusion and premise(s). Look first for the conclusion. The answers are given in the back of the book.

Example

Argument:	Shakespeare must have had formal schooling, because he was able to write, and he exhibited immense knowledge.

Diagram: Premises: 1. Shakespeare was able to write.
                         2. Shakespeare exhibited immense knowledge.
             _____
             Conclusion: Shakespeare must have had formal schooling.

1. Jake must be a communist, for he hangs around with communists.
2. The butler, because he was not at the house at the time, could not have killed the maid.
3. I've looked everywhere for a good used car, and I haven't found one.
4. Arch supports can actually lengthen your life, for they reduce pain and improve your disposition.
5. Lincoln is dead, because he was shot.
6. Because more babies are born every year and there is less and less food to feed them, there is sure to be a crisis in the near future.
7. If there is life on Jupiter, there is available oxygen there. But there is no available oxygen there; hence, there is no life on Jupiter.
8. All linguists speak at least two languages. It follows that Harvey speaks at least two languages, because he is a linguist.
9. You can't tell me that UFOs aren't real, at least some of them, any-

way. I mean, there's so much evidence. Just this morning I read in the newspaper that last year over 300 UFO sightings were reported.

10. Either they'll find a cure for AIDS, or there's going to be an epidemic. But it doesn't look as if they're going to find a cure for it, so there's sure to be an epidemic.

11. Collier must be the new president, because all the newspapers say he won the election.

12. Tom doesn't have ESP, because if he did, he would have known that his wife was being unfaithful, and he didn't.

13. In the spring the cotton needs harvesting, and lots of people crowd into this area for work. Sylvia can't stand crowds. Last year she took an early vacation just to escape all the people.

14. All newspapers distort facts to sell stories. For this reason you can never trust the newspapers.

15. Lizzy Borden was the only one home at the time her mother and father were murdered with an ax, so she's got to be the one who did it. The neighbors saw no one going to or coming from the house at the time.

16. If everyone were honest, we wouldn't need to put locks on our doors. But not everyone is honest, so we do have to put locks on our doors.

17. The act of abortion is not only the murder of an individual person, it is a crime against humanity. Anyone who is for abortion is an enemy of the human race.

II. Common Fallacies

Identify the fallacy committed in each of the following items. Some examples may contain more than one type of fallacy. The answers are given in the back of the book.

1. Yes, I [Franz Caber, a psychic counselor] admit that I lie to my clients occasionally, but so what? Oliver North admitted lying to *Congress!*

2. Two years ago I became mildly interested in the New Age movement, but it didn't really impress me until after I started to travel. Now that I've seen that the New Age movement has spread all over the world, I realize that there's got to be something to it; its ideas must be true.

3. Charles Berlitz does have his facts correct about the Bermuda Triangle. How do I know? Because to question him would be disrespectful.

4. Steve: The amazing "Dr. D" has a rare gift: she can see spirits.

   Ron: How do you know she can see spirits?

   Steve: Because she is not an ordinary person. She has unusual power.

5. Dead people who were murdered don't really care about vengeance; they won't ask you to punish or kill their murderer. I know this is true because Ms. Pring, my parapsychology teacher, told me.

6. We can see that our arms are connected to our bodies and that the limbs of a tree are connected to the trunk. But if we widen our purview, we can see that objects that are miles apart are connected by the space between them. Thus, everything in the universe is connected to everything else.

7. I wear my star sapphire to prevent a heart attack. It must work. I've never had a heart attack.

8. The Better Business Bureau has nothing on record to indicate that Kevin Ryerson (Shirley MacLaine's channeler) is a con artist. So, certainly he is not a con artist.

9. Morti Shawn says that psychic surgery is a scam, but I would question anything he says, because he's an alcoholic.

10. A recent poll showed that 72 percent of Americans believe that some people can know about events before they happen. This is very strong evidence that precognition is real.

11. Is Patti still allowing her skepticism to block her spiritual growth? Well, I never see her at any of our psychic fairs, so evidently she is.

12. Ben Harrah hasn't shown up at work for two weeks. What's going on? Has he been abducted by space aliens, or did he step into a time warp? I'm quite sure that he didn't step into a time warp, so he must have been abducted by space aliens.

13. We need data on ESP, and Robert Ferguson has offered to answer any questions we might have. But how can we trust him when he is a parapsychologist himself?

14. The people of Iceland believe in leprechauns. Some of their roads even go around the "houses" of leprechauns. The people of Iceland have been believing this way for centuries, so I think it is right and proper that they should carry on with this time-honored belief.

15. I've had my tarot cards read five times, and each time I got helpful

information from it. I tell you, whenever you go to a tarot reader, you're going to learn something important.

16. Dr. Thompson, the physician, says that crystals have no healing power, but that's nonsense. He's just saying that so you'll go to him with your ailments instead of using crystals.

17. Voodoo is an intriguing subject, and it can't be purely superstition, because just look at the millions of people who believe in it and practice it.

18. Skeptics have been trying to show that spiritualism is a fraud and that spirits don't exist. But it's obvious that spirits *do* exist. Just watch people, especially at Christmas or New Year. Practically everybody catches the spirit at those times.

19. After all this time there is not a shred of evidence of life in other parts of the universe. It is quite certain, then, that we are the only living creatures in the universe.

20. Two weeks ago I went to a psychic fair and had my aura cleansed. The next day I got an 'A' on my math test. Since I usually get 'C's in math, I know the aura cleansing made a big difference in my mathematical ability. The next time I've got a big, important test coming up, it's off for another cleansing for me!

21. Joan says that she has a ghost in her attic. She lived in that same house for over 10 years, so why is she just now seeing a ghost there? Obviously it's just her imagination acting up because she started reading horror novels.

22. Some scientists say that channeling is not real. That's because they think they know everything there is to know about the universe.

23. Marsha began taking powdered rhinoceros horn, and in no time at all she was enjoying sex again. That's proof that powdered rhinoceros horn is really an effective aphrodisiac.

24. In order to get proof that levitation is real, you've got to believe in it, because unless you think it's true, you'll never get convincing evidence.

25. Uriah Gomez, the psychic detective, told the ladies at the Women's League that investing in real estate guaranteed at least a 20 percent return on your money. So, it seems that real estate is a good place to put your money.

26. My sister was cheated by a psychic healer, and just this morning I read in the newspaper about an Arizona man who was conned out of his life savings by a so-called psychic. I'm never going to go near any kind of psychic person. They're all con artists.

27. Shirley MacLaine's book *Out on a Limb* must be factual. Look at how much money she's made from it.
28. Reincarnation is a fact, because every person has actually been through several previous lifetimes.
29. Many parapsychology professors have testified that evidence is accumulating that ESP is real, but remember that these same professors are the ones who receive grant money for research on this subject.
30. Thousands of people held hands and sang songs all over the world during the harmonic convergence. Shortly after that, Mikhail Gorbachev announced his policy of *glasnost*. You can see that our efforts during the harmonic convergence are bearing fruit already.
31. Trudy is critical of astrology, but that's because she doesn't understand it. I told her I wouldn't discuss it with her until she studied it. You can't knock an idea unless you know something about it.
32. Objects were mysteriously moving in the house. Either someone was moving them by psychokinesis, or it was ghosts. There was nothing to indicate that it was psychokinesis, so it had to be ghosts [Raymond Burr, in the movie *Psychic Phenomena*].
33. It would not be appropriate to invite Shirley MacLaine to the scientific conference, because scientists are devoted to using reason, and she doesn't believe in using reason.
34. Dietrich told the *Herald Examiner* yesterday that his wife could levitate. But this guy is a child molester, so I don't believe anything he says.
35. Arnaud: Aren't you taking advantage of people's ignorance when you sell them these worthless biorhythm charts?

    Bret: But how is this any different from the astrologer who sells people their horoscopes?
36. Bart: I'd marry Betty if it weren't for her practice of Satanism, which uses animal sacrifices.

    Nancy: But Betty has been doing that for 30 years. You can't expect her to stop now.
37. Professor: I've been studying parapsychology for 20 years now, and I've learned a great deal.

    Student: Then tell me, why do some people have more ESP ability than others?

CHAPTER 4

❏   ❏   ❏   ❏   ❏   ❏   ❏

The Paranormal

Extraordinary claims require extraordinary evidence.

Carl Sagan

What is the paranormal? This term applies to phenomena that apparently transcend the explanatory power of mainstream science and stem from unknown or hidden causes. The accompanying list represents only a portion of the phenomena called paranormal.

alien abductions	levitation	psychic
ancient astronauts	life after death	photographs
astral travel	Loch Ness monster	psychic predictions
astrology	mental telepathy	psychic readings
auras	moon madness	psychic surgery
Bermuda Triangle	numerology	psychokinesis
bigfoot	Ouija board	psychometry
biorhythms	palmistry	pyramid power
clairvoyance	past-life therapy	reincarnation
channeling	phrenology	seances
dowsing	plant consciousness	spontaneous human
fortune telling	precognition	combustion
ghosts	psychic detectives	table tipping
healing crystals	psychic healing	UFOs

Take psychokinesis, for example. For a person to actually bend a steel spoon with the power of his mind alone is, indeed, extraordinary. (Try it!) A young man from Israel named Uri Geller claimed to be able to do so, and he achieved fame and fortune through his numerous performances. He was tested by parapsychologists at the Stanford Research Institute (SRI) and was reported to have genuine psychic powers.

And what about extrasensory perception (ESP)? Many claim to have had the eerie experience of reading another person's mind (telepathy), knowing about a situation without being there (clairvoyance), or knowing about a situation before it happened (precognition). In the early 1930s J. B. Rhine began tests at Duke University on these phenomena. It was the first serious scientific attempt to verify the existence of ESP, and spectacular results were reported.

Still a third example of a paranormal phenomenon is the mysterious disappearance of ships and airplanes into thin air. It is said that such things do happen in an area off the Florida coast called the Bermuda Triangle (Berlitz, 1978).

❏ Investigating the Paranormal

Although reports of extraordinary phenomena naturally tax our credulity and leave us hanging in a quandary of wonder and debate, it is important to remember that the universe is not obliged to conform to our expectations or even to the limits of our imagination. Thus, we cannot know that an extraordinary claim is false (or true) before careful investigation. We must keep an open mind to the possibility that a wild claim is true. The only exception is a claim that is contradictory (paradoxical) or unintelligible. We will cover this case when we discuss the possible versus the impossible.

Scientific Skepticism

Scientists would readily agree that we do not know everything and that almost anything is possible, and yet they remain skeptical of paranormal phenomena. Why? We can answer this question with three words: *no solid evidence*. When we examine the evidence, we invariably meet with disappointment.

Take, for example, the testing done on Geller at the SRI. (Incidently, the SRI has nothing to do with Stanford University.) Geller was tested for a variety of psychic powers, including psychokinesis and mental telepathy. He was allowed to interrupt or discontinue any of the tests at any time for any reason, for example, headaches, nature calls, and so on. This leeway alone invalidates the tests, but there's more. During his telepathy tests, he made frequent trips to the bathroom and was allowed to pass through the room where the sender (from whom Geller was attempting to receive telepathic messages) and the target image were located. This made it extremely easy for him to get a look at the target image. Moreover, there was a hole in the wall dividing the two rooms where the sender and receiver were stationed. The lack of adequate controls at the SRI made cheating extremely easy, making the data coming from that laboratory totally unacceptable (Randi, 1975).

Geller began as a nightclub magician in Israel, but he soon realized that he could draw a much larger crowd and make a lot more money if he billed himself as a "psychic." He did this until the law and pressure from the Israeli authorities forced him to discontinue his show. He then came to the United States and made a fortune performing as a psychic. He is willing to be tested by scientists but refuses to be tested by magicians. This alone should arouse suspicion in a critical mind. But beyond this, Geller's sleight-of-hand methods have been clearly observed by magicians, and his acts of cheating have even been captured on film. Skilled magicians can duplicate all of his illusions, and his manager has testified that Geller uses an accomplice in trickery. Geller is probably the most thoroughly exposed charlatan of all time, but he is still hailed by many believers as a genuine psychic (Diaconis, 1985).

We meet with a similar disappointment when we research the studies in parapsychology undertaken by Rhine at Duke. The laboratory would occasionally get impressive results, but none of them could be repeated (an important requirement for valid science). Moreover, Walter J. Levy, the director of Rhine's laboratory, was caught faking records to make it appear that positive results had been achieved (Coon, 1986). This, it turns out, is not uncommon news about parapsychology laboratories.

Fraud and Project Alpha

But the problem is not just that some researchers are dishonest. An even greater problem is that fraud is rampant in this field, and honest scientists often do not design experiments to prevent it. In 1979 James Randi, a professional magician, began his Project Alpha experiment in which two young magicians, Mike Edwards and Steve Shaw, posing as psychics, went to the parapsychology laboratory at Washington University in St. Louis to be tested (Randi, 1983). By using sleight-of-hand and simple conjuring routines, the two magicians were able to convince the researchers that they had psychic power.

Over a period of two years the two young men were tested at several laboratories in the United States and abroad, and they were praised as the world's best psychics. The project was finally brought to an end at a press conference in which Edwards and Shaw announced that they were merely magicians and that all their wonders were conjuring acts. It was extremely easy, they said, to fool the researchers. They also explained that they had been instructed by Randi to admit immediately that they were using fakery if they were ever asked. They were never asked!

Project Alpha should give us pause the next time we read about a scientific study that claims to prove the existence of ESP. In fact, because of Project Alpha, many scientists now realize that magicians, not scientists, are much better qualified to judge whether ESP is actually taking place.

The Bermuda Triangle

Many books have been written (and royalties made) on the Bermuda Triangle mystery. Do ships and aircraft really just disappear? Lawrence Kusche, a librarian, took an interest in the bizarre reports and began investigating them. He soon found himself involved in a project that took him all over the world to libraries, military installations, shipping companies, and homes and offices for personal interviews. His findings: each of the popular accounts either didn't happen the way it had been reported, didn't happen where it had been reported to have happened, or didn't happen at all. His conclusion: the Bermuda Triangle mystery is a hoax (Kusche, 1975).

The television series *Nova* corroborated Kusche's findings. One show featured interviews with the air traffic controllers who had been in touch with the pilots of five bombers that disappeared on a training mission in December 1945. The discrepancy between their account and the popular account was striking. According to the popular account the patrol leader radioed back that the pilots were lost, that they didn't know which way was west, that everything was strange, and that even the ocean didn't look as it should. And then . . . silence.

But in fact there was no mystery about what had happened and why it had happened. Records of the radio communications show that contact was not lost at all. The pilots became uncertain about their location. They were not sure whether they were on the east or west side of the Florida peninsula, and they changed direction several times looking for an identifiable landmark. At one point they headed north, thinking that this would take them out of the Gulf of Mexico and put them over land. Unfortunately, they were actually east of the peninsula, and their new direction simply carried them farther north over the Atlantic Ocean. The weather turned bad, the planes eventually ran out of fuel, and the pilots had to ditch their aircraft in the ocean on a dark, stormy night, hundreds of miles outside of the Bermuda Triangle!

Myth: Scientists refuse to consider things they don't understand.

Scientists are skeptical not because they don't understand these phenomena. On the contrary, scientists are constantly confronted with things that they don't understand; they make their living trying to discover the causes. The objective of science is to discover the nature of reality whatever it might be, no matter how weird. And scientists *have* looked seriously at paranormal claims. If they remain skeptical, it is because the evidence does not support the claims made, not because scientists cannot explain them. In other words, it's not that scientists don't understand mental telepathy; it's that they have no reason to think that telepathy exists.

CSICOP

Paranormal claims are extremely common, and it is fortunate that there is an organization devoted to investigating them. It is called the Committee for the Scientific Investigation of Claims of the Paranormal (CSICOP), and it was formed in 1976 by Paul Kurtz, a philosopher at the State University of New York, Buffalo. The committee is a group of dedicated individuals from a wide range of disciplines. Its ranks include the astronomer Carl Sagan, the author and biochemist Isaac Asimov, the psychologist B. F. Skinner, the magician and author James Randi, the philosopher Sidney Hook, the scientist and two-time Nobel laureate Murray Gell-Mann, the scientist Paul MacCready, the philosopher W. V. Quine, the magician and columnist Henry Gordon, the biologist Stephen J. Gould, the science writer Martin Gardner, the biophysicist and codiscoverer of the DNA molecule Francis Crick, and many other prominent intellectuals.

The committee is pledged to investigate paranormal claims from a scientific point of view and to publish its findings. It does not reject paranormal claims before investigating them but seeks to examine them objectively and carefully. It maintains a data base of information available to the general public, and its official publication is the quarterly magazine the *Skeptical Inquirer*.

❑ The Possible versus the Impossible

Earlier, I said that almost anything is possible, and I should now clarify that statement. Though we want to keep our minds open to even the most far-fetched possibilities, some popular ideas must be rejected because they are paradoxical (see Chapter 2); that is, they contain a contradiction and, consequently, make no sense. It might be better to say:

> Anything that we can describe without contradiction is possible.
> Or:
> Anything that makes sense is possible.

Logical Impossibility

When something is impossible because it's contradictory, it is called a logical impossibility. The square circle, as we defined it in Chapter 2, is logically impossible. So, too, is a married bachelor. Recall that a contradiction is fundamentally nonsensical, and for this reason asserting the reality or possibility of any such idea is a fallacy. Let's call this the *Fallacy of Affirming a Logical Impossibility*. The basic form looks like this:

> X exists (or might exist) [when X is a logical impossibility].

Now we must ask: are any paranormal phenomena logically impossible? That is, do any of the concepts that people mention when discussing the paranormal involve a contradiction? If so, we can dismiss them at once as being pointless to investigate, because they are nonsensical. One example that suggests itself is precognition.

Precognition   Precognition, by definition, is knowing what the future actually has in store. Of course, anyone can have a feeling or a hunch that comes true. This can happen by educated guessing or by chance. But can a person actually *know* what's coming without using information provided to the five senses? Shall we include this among other numerous possibilities, or does the idea involve a contradiction that makes it nonsensical?

To know now about what hasn't happened yet might sound possible, but perhaps this is just because we have heard people verbalize the idea so often. Actually, if we analyze it carefully, we can find a contradiction in it. Knowing now about something that hasn't happened yet is rather like seeing before our eyes something that is not before our eyes. (Of course, we can do this in the imagination or on a video screen, but in these cases we are not literally seeing the genuine article.) To literally see before our eyes what is not before our eyes is a contradiction.

In the same way, to be aware now of what has not taken place yet is a contradiction. (Of course, we can have hunches and imaginings that come true, but in these cases we are not literally aware of that future event.) What hasn't happened yet cannot be literally present to anyone's mind now, because it doesn't exist yet. Thus, precognition, strictly speaking, is a contradictory idea, and to speak of precognition as a fact or even as a possibility is to commit the Fallacy of Affirming a Logical Impossibility.

One way of seeing that the notion of precognition is nonsense is to carry out the following thought experiment. Let's say that you have a precognition that you are going to be in an accident on the freeway tomorrow. You could, if you wanted, simply stay in bed all day tomorrow and falsify your own precognition. Your precognition puts you in a position of being able to prevent what will happen! But this is a contradiction: if it will happen, you cannot prevent it, and if you know about it, you can do something to prevent it. (For a deeper discussion of this topic, see the Appendix, item 4.)

Time Travel   Another example of a popular idea that is logically impossible is time travel. If I could actually go into tomorrow today (here we already have a contradiction), I would experience happening now what is not happening now, and this is a contradiction. Or if I went forward in time 300 years, I would be living in a time in which I was no longer living (a contradiction)! And what about going backward in time? If I went back to a point in time before I was born (already a contradiction), I could arrange it so my parents would never meet! I (an existing being) could bring it about that I never existed. Thus, we can see that time travel is a very paradoxical notion.

One of my favorite television shows was *The Twilight Zone,* and one of my favorite themes was time travel. I can enjoy this theme even when I know it's logical nonsense. It's a lot of fun to see someone in 1961 go back to 1 million B.C. But what I'm actually seeing are just changes of scenery occurring one after another. I, the viewer, am invited to collaborate with the writer of the story by using my imagination to interpret a change in scenery as a trip through time. This is logical nonsense, but it's fun.

Precognition and time travel, then, are notions that we can discard because they are nonsense. There is no point in saying, "Well, maybe someday our minds will be capable of precognition." This would be like saying, "Maybe someday our minds will be capable of mnbjibwrl." And there is no point in saying, "Well, maybe our technology will make time travel possible," because the notion of time travel is, likewise, nonsense. If a concept is unintelligible, so, too, is the idea that someday it might be possible. Moreover, if a concept is unintelligible, scientific efforts to validate it are a waste of valuable resources.

Physical Impossibility

We must be careful to distinguish the logically impossible from what is enormously difficult or physically impossible. Can you imagine jumping over the Empire State Building? This is something that lies beyond the range of our physical power; it is physically impossible. We simply don't have enough strength to do it. If we did have this power, however, we could do it. It's conceivable that a new superfood could come along that would give us this ability or that special injections in our muscles would make them equal to the task. There's nothing inconceivable about jumping over the Empire State Building, and there's no contradiction involved in describing it. Though it is (at present) physically impossible, it is not logically impossible.

When Do We Need to Investigate?

If you were told that someone had jumped over the Empire State Building without any artificial assistance, you'd be right to be skeptical; given our present understanding of the human body, it is highly improbable. But in order to really know whether the story is true, you would have to investigate it. If you were told that there was a person who could read minds, you would be right to be skeptical, because an actual case of mental telepathy has never been established. But, again, you would have to investigate to know for sure; like most other paranormal ideas, it is logically possible.

If, on the other hand, you were told that someone had made a time machine or had seen into the future, you would be right to reject this claim without investigation, because it is logically impossible. That is to say, it involves a contradiction and actually makes no sense.

Long before the Wright brothers came along, Leonardo da Vinci believed that machines could be made that would enable human beings to fly. In spite of the scorn of numerous skeptics he sketched many designs and even made prototype flying machines. Unfortunately, his machines were never successful, but Leonardo never gave up trying, because he realized that there was nothing physically impossible about it. Birds, obviously, could fly, and they were heavier than air. But if Leonardo had thought that such flight was logically impossible, he probably would not have tried.

The possibilities that we must keep an open mind about, then, are the logical ones, the ones that make sense. These are the only ideas that we can profitably discuss, and they are the only ones for which proof could conceivably be obtained.

❑ Who Has the Burden of Proof?

Whose job is it to provide proof when a paranormal claim is made, the believer's or the skeptic's? Is it reasonable to demand that people who claim to have been abducted by aliens from another world prove their case? Or is it the other way around? Perhaps, if claimants are credible, we should believe their story until it is disproven.

When skeptics and believers argue about the paranormal, they often come to a stalemate like this:

Joe: Prove that bigfoot exists.

Jim: Prove that it doesn't!

In this dispute, it may seem that Joe and Jim are even, since neither can prove his case. But wait a minute. Are their demands equally reasonable? If bigfoot exists, there's a chance that Jim could prove it, if he wants to spend enough time, effort, and money to do so. But if bigfoot does not exist, how could Joe ever prove it? There is really nothing Joe or anyone else could do to prove that bigfoot does not exist. Therefore, Joe's demand is reasonable, but Jim's demand is not.

Jim is making an error in reasoning called the *Fallacy of Demanding*

Proof of a Negative. This error is made when a person asks for evidence of the nonexistence of something. The basic form is:

Prove that X does not exist.

To understand why this is a fallacy, let's consider griffins. A griffin is a creature from Greek mythology, half lion and half eagle. Here we have an example of something that we have every reason to think does not exist. But do we have proof? Could we ever get proof? Of course we can say that it is a mythological creature and that no one has ever seen one in the real world, but this in no way proves that griffins do not exist.

Let's look more closely at the difference between a positive proposition and a negative one:

A: Griffins exist. (positive)
B: Griffins do not exist. (negative)

If proposition A (a positive statement) is true, proof that it is true is at least possible. That is, we might someday come across such a creature, or a whole population of them, and this would prove that proposition A is true.

But what about proposition B (a negative statement)? If this proposition is true, we can never look forward to a day when proof of it will emerge, and there is nothing that you (or anyone) can do to show that it is true. The best you can do is to show that there is no good reason to believe that A is true (for example, by pointing out that griffins occur only in mythical literature and that no one has ever seen one in the real world). But this does not actually prove that proposition B is true, nor could anything do so. Thus, it is for very good reason that scientists say,

You can't prove a negative.

Has Science Proved That ESP Does Not Exist?

For many decades scientists have endeavored to prove that ESP is real, but so far they have not succeeded. This is why most scientists think that there is no such thing. But have they proved that ESP does not exist?

What could prove that ESP does not exist? Now, it is very clear what would prove that ESP *does* exist. If a person consistently scored 99 percent on carefully controlled ESP tests for several years under conditions precluding the possibility of cheating and could perform for skeptics as well as believers, this would be convincing evidence of ESP.

But what test or series of tests could we devise to prove that no one had ESP? If everyone in the world were tested for ESP and failed, would this prove that ESP did not exist? No, because there is always the possibility that ESP was not active at the time of the test.

In our discussion of the paranormal it would be a mistake to think that science has proved that ESP or bigfoot does not exist. This would be attempting the impossible. Rather, what scientific investigation has revealed is that there is, so far, no substantial evidence for these phenomena; hence, there is no reason to think that they exist. But this is very different from proving that they don't. There can be no such proof. (Actually, some negative propositions *can* be proved; see the Appendix, item 5.)

The fact that negatives can't usually be proved is one important reason why the burden of proof rests with the person who makes the extraordinary claim. Thus, Jim has a burden of proof, but Joe does not. If Jim cannot produce strong evidence of bigfoot, Joe simply has no reason to believe that bigfoot exists.

There is another good reason why the burden of proof rests with the person making the claim: human fallibility. Because hoaxes are common and human powers of perception and reasoning are vulnerable to error, it is right that we should remain skeptical until strong evidence is in. This posture is necessary if we want to sort fact from fiction.

Hume's Scale

In the 18th century the philosopher David Hume described a method for dealing intelligently with paranormal stories:

> When anyone tells me he saw a dead man restored to life, I immediately consider with myself, whether it be more probable that this person should either deceive or be deceived, or that the fact, which he relates, should have really happened. I weigh the one miracle against the other. (Hume, 1975, p. 116)

In other words, a rational person will respond to a paranormal story by asking this question: is it more likely that the laws of nature have gone haywire or that human beings have bent the facts? The obvious answer is that it is vastly more probable, judging from past experience, that humans have distorted the facts. After all, human deceit and fallibility are everyday things, but paranormal claims have never been authenticated. (If they had, they wouldn't be called paranormal!)

Notice that Hume is not saying that a paranormal claim can't be true, only that it is very probably false and that it is not reasonable to believe it. This is another way of saying that testimony simply is not good enough to establish any paranormal claim. Hume is reminding us that we should demand good evidence.

❏ Factors Explaining Belief in the Paranormal

If there really is no persuasive evidence supporting paranormal phenomena, why do so many people believe in them? I'll attempt to answer this question in terms of three (overlapping) factors: (1) a popular philosophy, (2) environmental influences, and (3) psychological tendencies that promote fallacious reasoning.

A Popular Philosophy

There are a number of beliefs that, for many people, provide the foundation for belief in the paranormal. Here are some often heard:

1. We can't be certain of anything. We don't really know anything. Nothing is certain.
2. Some things simply cannot be proved scientifically, for example, love.
3. Scientists don't know everything.
4. There are things we just can't know.
5. Our senses are limited.
6. The mind is a mysterious entity; we do not know its limits.
7. It's not good to be too skeptical, because anything is possible.
8. Everything is relative: if a person believes in something, it's true for that person; and if he or she doesn't believe in it, it isn't true for that person.

These are very popular ideas that are often taken as signs of intellectual sophistication in the person who embraces them. They are also tools frequently used to defend belief in paranormal phenomena. If we can't be certain of anything and anything is possible, it would seem that only a closed mind would be skeptical about paranormal matters. Such a person would be assuming that we already know everything or that what exists is limited to what we can know. And if some things cannot be proved scientifically, perhaps we shouldn't expect to get proof of paranormal things.

Is this correct reasoning? Let us analyze this philosophy item by item.

"We Can't Be Certain of Anything" Let's suppose that this is true, that is, that nothing is certain. We will still need to rank some claims as more certain (or less uncertain) than others. For example, I am far more certain that there is a restaurant at the north end of my block than I am that George Washington chopped down his father's cherry tree. Similarly, an actual demonstration of levitation would make us far more certain that this phenomenon was real than a mere report of it.

So, even if we grant that nothing is certain, we would still feel that our level of uncertainty was substantially reduced if, after only hearing reports of levitation, we actually got to see it. Such a demonstration, especially if it were repeated under proper observing conditions, would reduce our level of uncertainty enough to authenticate levitation. (For further analysis of this issue see the Appendix, item 6.)

"Some Things Cannot Be Proved Scientifically" It is true for science that only publicly observable, quantifiable data count as evidence for any claim. If love is defined as affectionate, caring, concerned behavior, its existence can be observed and verified. If, on the other hand, we define love as a private, subjective state of consciousness, it ceases to be a topic that science deals with. It's not that science cannot prove that this type of love exists but that love defined in this way is simply not a subject for scientific investigation. There are many issues that science does not deal with (see the next chapter). Not all questions are scientific ones.

Nevertheless, many paranormal phenomena could be proved scientifically, if they existed. For example, if someone claims to have the ability to "see" through solid concrete walls, this claim can easily be verified by observing a demonstration. We can do the same thing with mental telepathy, psychokinesis, and most of the other things listed at the beginning of this chapter.

"Scientists Don't Know Everything" It is a well-known cliché that the more we learn, the more we discover our ignorance. In fact, a scientist would be the first to admit that there are things we don't know. After all, it is the job of the scientist to investigate, explore, and discover. Any scientific endeavor whatsoever springs from the premise that we don't know everything.

"There Are Things We Just Can't Know" It would be presumptuous to deny the claim that some things can't be known, but such a claim is either irrelevant or false. If it refers to things that have never been experienced by anyone and could never be experienced by anyone, it points to things that do not and could not ever concern us. On the other hand, if it refers to things that people claim to experience—for example, mental telepathy—it is false, for we can test and confirm mental telepathy if it does indeed occur.

"Our Senses Are Limited" Even though modern technology has greatly expanded our ability to know the universe (for example, by the use of telescopes and microscopes), our capacity to know is still limited. But we do not need infinite powers of cognition in order to discern whether a person is levitating or has ESP or whether ships do disappear into oblivion in the Bermuda Triangle.

"The Mind Is a Mysterious Entity" Even if we grant that the mind is a mysterious entity (which is questionable; see Chapter 1), we are still going to need hard evidence that it is capable of ESP or astral travel. Moreover, from the fact that we are ignorant of the workings of the mind, it does not follow that it is capable of paranormal acts. (For further discussion, see the Appendix, item 7.)

"It's Not Good to Be Too Skeptical, Because Anything Is Possible" It's true that if we're closed minded, we might miss an opportunity to discover something important. But it is a mistake to think that being skeptical is being closed-minded. A healthy skepticism is simply one that insists on good evidence before accepting an extraordinary claim. This is our protection against fraud and deceit. One of the most certain indications that something phony is going on is when our skepticism is viewed with disdain. If this happens, we have excellent reason to be suspicious.

"Everything Is Relative" Is it really true that *everything* is relative? Clearly, some things are. For example, suppose I say, "A fresh, tree-ripened apricot is the most delicious fruit in the world." Now, this *is* a

relative matter. It's true for me, but it may not be true for anyone else. Belief in ghosts may also be relative in this way. If I believe in ghosts, then when I walk into a dark, old, abandoned building, I may see apparitions that others don't see.

But surely many claims are not relative in this way at all—for example, that there is a fig tree in my backyard and that an atomic bomb was dropped on Hiroshima. These are publicly observable things, and they aren't true just for me. Similarly, mental telepathy, clairvoyance, and levitation really occur, or they don't. If they really do occur, they can be publicly demonstrated and observed.

The Value of the Popular Philosophy The "popular philosophy," as I've called it, springs from our natural desire to know and understand the universe, and it provides us with some excellent principles to guide our inquiry: we should not be closed minded; we do not know everything; anything is possible. But on the other hand, being open minded and being humble about our knowledge does not mean that we should stop thinking critically. If we really want knowledge (as opposed to mere belief), we will have to ask questions and scrutinize the claims that are made. And the more unusual the claim, the greater the need for evidence. Having an open mind is not the same as having a blank mind, and sensational stories are no substitute for hard evidence provided by careful observation and testing.

Environmental Influences

Many of the factors that contribute to the widespread belief in the paranormal are largely outside of our control. We will consider three of them: the media, misinformation, and ignorance.

The Media Television stations and newspapers are eager to report that a psychic is helping the police department capture a criminal, that lamps are crashing to the floor because of a poltergeist, or that UFOs have been seen in Florida. But they are not so anxious to tell us when an exciting story turns out to be a hoax. The reason that reporters do this is easy to find: Hearing that UFOs are not real is not nearly as interesting as hearing that they are. And reading about psychic detective work is exciting, but reading about psychic failures is boring.

The effect on the public mind is predictable: If the police department is using psychics, there must really be people who actually have psychic power. And if UFOs were really observed, then . . . In fact, I've had many people tell me that they believe in psychics because the police department makes use of them. What we must bear in mind whenever we see a story like this is that a newspaper or a television station is a business, and in order to stay in business it must present stories that will capture public interest.

When Dorothy Allison was called in by the police department of Atlanta to apply her psychic talents in solving a series of child murders, many newspapers and television stations announced this fact. What they didn't report was the outcome: the police admitted that they had yielded to public pressure in hiring Allison and that the 42 leads she had given them had come to nothing (Randi, 1982–1983). The media have little incentive to report this type of information, because it is unexciting.

But there is an important lesson to be learned here: We are systematically misled by the media into thinking that many paranormal claims are true. We are misled not only by deliberate misinformation but also by getting only half the story. In this way a national and even global illusion is created that psychic phenomena are common and that paranormal events are real. It's no wonder, then, that a charlatan like Geller can be exposed as a fraud and yet continue to enjoy fame and fortune.

Misinformation Part of the problem, too, is often that what we think we know simply isn't true. Take, for example, the notion that we use only 10 percent of our brain. Since we use only 10 percent of our brain (the argument goes), we should not be skeptical about ESP, because it's just possible that some people enjoy the advantage of using a portion of their brain that the rest of us don't.

Myth: We use only 10 percent of our brain.

But this idea is just a popular myth. If it were true we only used 10 percent of our brain, we should expect to find large areas of cells or numerous individual cells in the brain with no identifiable function at all. But this is far from true. Physiological psychologists have mapped out the function of practically every portion of the brain, and they have found no vacant areas at all.

It is true, however, that many of us could probably be more intelligent than we are. Comparative studies have shown (other things being equal) that children raised in a highly stimulating environment are brighter than other children. Similar studies with rats show that the brain is thicker, heavier, and more developed if early environmental stimulation is provided. But the differences we are talking about here are nothing close to tenfold differences, and they have nothing to do with ESP.

Myth: People under hypnosis can't lie.

Another example of how misinformation can lead us astray is found in the recent UFO abduction craze. (This craze is fueled, apparently, by the long-standing myth that there is a government cover-up of actual UFO contacts; see Klass, 1983.) It is believed that when a hypnotized person relates a detailed story about having been taken aboard a flying saucer, the story must be true. But this is just another myth.

Experts in hypnosis have demonstrated that hypnosis easily gives rise to fantasy and *confabulation* (Hilgard, 1981). Confabulation is the process of creating pseudomemories. Thus, a person can concoct a detailed story about being abducted by aliens onto a flying saucer and come to believe that it really happened. (For a skeptical investigation into many well-known abduction cases see Klass, 1988.)

Ignorance   Many people view events as paranormal only because they are unaware of the factors that explain those events. An example is *firewalking,* the practice of walking barefoot on red-hot embers.

Actually, firewalking is something anyone can do, and this ability is explained by the difference between heat and temperature. Because your foot has more mass than the embers, the surface temperature of the embers drops dramatically (for a brief period) when contacted by your foot. Thus, it is possible to walk for a distance of about 15 feet on the embers. You're going to get burned, however, if you attempt to walk farther than this distance or if you try to stand on the embers for an equivalent amount of time.

A similar thing happens when you briefly stick your hand into (the air portion of) the oven after it has been on for one hour at 350 degrees. No harm. But if you should touch the inner surface of the oven walls, ouch! The air and the walls are at the same temperature, but because the siding has much more mass, it has much more heat to transfer to your hand than the air does. Consequently, instead of your hand causing the metal surface to cool down, the metal surface causes your hand to heat up.

Another example of the role of ignorance involves *dowsing,* the process of walking across a stretch of ground while holding a stick in order to locate a subterranean water source. Dowsing is still widely practiced. In fact, two of my students reported that they had actually experienced it themselves. But the fact remains that dowsing has been tested many times and has consistently failed.

During an appearance on the *Johnny Carson Show* in 1985, James Randi reported that he and Dick Smith had offered a $120,000 prize to anyone who could successfully pass a dowsing test. They buried 10 pipes in a plot of ground in Australia, but only one of them had water flowing through it at any given time. The dowsers were required to find the active pipe on each trial. Before the test, the dowsers said that they felt confident that they could score 100 percent on this test. In 500 trials they scored a mere 11 percent, very close to what would be expected by chance—10 percent.

The reason that dowsing seems to work, and the reason that there are many successful professional dowsers, is that if you drill deep enough, you can hit water just about anywhere. People continue to believe that dowsing works because they are unaware of the pervasiveness of subterranean streams and aquifers.

Another little-known fact that explains a lot is that a significant number of all problems for which people seek medical treatment are self-terminating. In other words, *many of the cases that doctors treat would cure themselves.* This includes everything from the common cold to cancer. It is therefore very easy to understand why there are numerous factual accounts of people actually getting better after receiving useless treatments. It's important to remember that just because you got better after getting treatment doesn't necessarily mean that the treatment cured you. (To determine this you need to do a controlled study. See the next chapter.)

To make matters even worse, some of the diseases that medical science is powerless to cure are also known to self-terminate (for example, some forms of cancer). Such cases are rare, but they do happen. If such a spontaneous reversal of the disease occurs while a useless treatment is being undertaken (for example, faith healing or bogus medicine), it will look as though the treatment cured the disease. These are remarkable cases, and when they occur, they usually get a lot of media attention. As we saw in Chapter 3, *Life* magazine ran a story about a man who had "cured" his cancer by eating nothing but grain foods for six months. The man, of course, was totally convinced that his diet had cured his cancer. (This is the Fallacy of False Cause.)

Closely associated with these statistical facts is something called the *placebo effect.* The Latin word *placebo* means "I shall please." The effect consists of taking an inert substance (one that has no medicinal value) prescribed by a doctor and getting better anyway. The reason that you get better is because you *believe* you will, and this improved attitude has a healing effect on the body. The effect is real, not imaginary; but it is the mind that cures, not the medication.

Not all diseases can be cured by the placebo effect, of course, but those that can provide an abundance of "proof" for quack "cures."

Ignorance also plays an important role when we are impressed by a dream that comes true. These are often called *precognitive dreams*. Many people think that such an event illustrates precognition. But actually we don't need anything paranormal to explain it; all we need are some facts about dreaming. Most of us don't realize that (1) we spend at least two hours each night dreaming and (2) we dream mostly about familiar people and situations. These two facts mean that it is extremely likely that at least once in our life we will have a dream that corresponds strikingly with a later event (Abell and Singer, 1981). If you take an informal poll of your friends and associates, you'll find that this occurrence is really quite common. Whenever I survey my classes with this question, I find that at least 50 percent of the students report having had a dream come true.

Some people claim to have memories of past lives, and thus life after (and before) death seems to be demonstrated. But these memory impressions can be explained by the phenomenon known as *cryptomnesia* (Harris, 1986). Cryptomnesia occurs when you (unconsciously) piece together a story from information acquired earlier from books, movies, newspapers, magazines, radio, television, and other people. The reemergence of these data seems baffling to you because it occurs spontaneously, and its origins are completely forgotten.

A classic example of this phenomenon occurred in 1952 when Virginia Tighe, a housewife in Pueblo, Colorado, began talking (under hypnosis) in an Irish brogue about her life in 19th-century Ireland as a person named Bridey Murphy (Gardner, 1957). Some time later (after *The Search for Bridey Murphy* had topped the best-seller list and tens of thousands of records of Tighe's trance sessions had been sold), it was found that she had had an Irish neighbor whose maiden name was Bridey Murphy. Gradually all of the details from her "past life" were found to derive from her real-life experiences as a girl growing up in Chicago. People ignorant of the phenomenon of cryptomnesia had been easily convinced that this was a case of reincarnation.

People are often impressed with what they hear because scientific terminology is used. Because they are not scientists themselves, they don't realize that the words don't make scientific sense. Here are some examples:

> The energy emanating from the psychic surgeon's fingers is super-high-frequency Kirlian waves [from the film *Mondo Magic*].

> [It] . . . requires to lower the vibratory frequency into what is called gaseous matter . . . to assume what is termed positive/negative fields of polarities. [Penny Torres, speaking as Mafu, is answering the question "How is channeling accomplished?" Mafu is supposed to be a spirit entity whose last physical embodiment was in first-century Pompeii.]

> Mafu is real because he has been tested with an oscilloscope [a follower of Penny Torres—Mafu].

Any of these statements would cause hysterical laughter in a knowledgeable scientist. But to someone who wants to believe and is ignorant of science, they can sound impressive.

If you stare at a stationary spot of light in a dark room, the light will appear to move. The movements can vary from sudden jerks to oscillations to swoopings in a definite direction. The effect is produced only when the room is dark enough to obscure any frame of reference that would show the light to be stationary. This phenomenon is called the *autokinetic effect* and is the probable explanation of a spot of light seen in the night sky as a rapidly moving UFO (Bartholomew, 1990). Pilots are aware of this effect, and to eliminate it, they will line up a distant beacon with the border of the windshield.

Five million people go each year to a river that flows near a church in Lourdes, France, to be cured of their ailments. Fifty years ago 5,000 cures were accepted as inexplicable; but from 1947 to 1980 only 28 were pronounced official. To date, the Lourdes Medical Bureau officially recognizes a total of just 64 cures since people began going there in the middle 1800s (Bernstein, 1982). As our medical knowledge grows, fewer and fewer recoveries are viewed as miraculous. This clearly indicates that we perceive something as miraculous because we are ignorant of its natural causes.

Psychological Tendencies

There can be no doubt that human psychology itself is part of the reason that many people believe in paranormal phenomena. We will examine nine universal tendencies that seem especially important, because they can, and frequently do, lead us to reason badly on paranormal issues. Let's begin with a list of these traits and the fallacies that often attend them:

1. Tendency: We enjoy an exciting story.
   Fallacy: jumping to fantastic conclusions
2. Tendency: We are prone to wishful thinking.
   Fallacy: deriving fact from possibility
   Fallacy: doublethink
3. Tendency: We see a causal connection where none exists.
   Fallacy: explaining a coincidence
   Fallacy: the gambler
4. Tendency: We need self-respect.
   Fallacy: rationalization
5. Tendency: We have confidence in what we see.
   Fallacy: seeing is believing
6. Tendency: We have confidence in what we feel.
   Fallacy: deriving "it is" from "it seems"
7. Tendency: We are inconsistent observers.
   Fallacy: selective perception
8. Tendency: We are prone to interpretation.
   Fallacy: projected specifics
9. Tendency: We are often naive.
   Fallacy: the egocentric fallacy

We Enjoy an Exciting Story   As I pointed out earlier, the fact that people enjoy paranormal stories is the reason that we frequently encounter them in the media. The simple truth is that nobody likes to be bored, and this may be the reason that, when left to our own devices, we often prefer an extraordinary explanation to an ordinary one.

In 1872 the *Mary Celeste,* a two-masted cargo ship, was found drifting crewless between Portugal and the Azores. Everything seemed to be in good order on board, but there was no trace of the crew of 11. Those on board never turned up, and no one knows how to explain this strange incident. It remains perhaps the greatest sea mystery in history. It is also one of the numerous cases that are included in the popular accounts of the Bermuda Triangle, even though it occurred nowhere near the triangle.

How can we explain it? Here's one possibility: the crew was abducted by extraterrestrials and taken away in a flying saucer to another galaxy. Of course, there is nothing impossible about this explanation, and it might even be true. But do we have good reason to accept it? No, because there is no convincing evidence of flying saucers (Klass, 1983), and we do have numerous other ways of explaining it in terms of ordinary causes.

When a mysterious event occurs and we are searching for an explanation, it is a mistake to begin with an extraordinary reason before considering an ordinary one. It is logical to begin with what is known, because it is more probable. To begin with a farfetched idea is called the *Fallacy of Jumping to Fantastic Conclusions,* and it looks like this:

Premise: X is a mystery.
_____

Conclusion: Therefore, X has a mysterious cause.

To avoid this fallacy, we should try to think of ordinary possibilities or unusual combinations of ordinary possibilities. An ordinary explanation for the *Mary Celeste* mystery, for example, is that everybody on board went for a swim at the same time (not realizing that no one was left on board), and a wind came up and pushed the ship away, leaving the people to the sharks. Or perhaps the people were abducted by pirates who murdered them and tossed them into the sea. Or . . . Obviously, there are numerous mundane possibilities that we should investigate before we think seriously about the flying saucer explanation.

The experience of *déjà vu* ("already seen," in French) often inspires people to jump to fantastic conclusions. It is the seeming memory of an experience that is actually happening for the first time. When it occurs, it can be accompanied by a feeling of familiarity so strong that it leads some people to believe that they actually were in that place in a previous lifetime. Thus, the experience is often taken as strong evidence of reincarnation.

"How else can you explain it?" one student asked. She was jumping to a fantastic conclusion, because she had made little or no effort to find an alternative explanation in terms of known phenomena. Actually, it isn't difficult to think of several ordinary ways to account for déjà vu. For example, maybe the new place closely resembles another place the person has been to. Or it may resemble a mental image conjured up when a story was read to her as a child. What about her dream images? It could resemble one of them. Then there are pictures from magazines, newspapers, television, and the movies. In a lifetime a person experiences millions of pictures; and encountering a scene that resembles one of them could easily create a feeling of familiarity.

Still another possible explanation (taken seriously by some psychologists) is that the new experience somehow registers in memory before we are consciously aware of it and so presents itself as something remembered. Clearly there are numerous ordinary possibilities that we should investigate before we even start talking about reincarnation as an explanation.

We Are Prone to Wishful Thinking   Another tendency that nourishes belief in the paranormal is that we want certain favorite beliefs to be true. When this desire is very strong, we give assent to weak arguments and disdain strong ones, and practically nothing can change our mind.

Sometimes a person who has been "dead" for a number of minutes is revived and reports having had experiences during the death interval. Such reports seem to indicate that there is conscious activity after death. The fact that many *near-death experiences* (NDEs) are described in the same way (as going through a dark tunnel and seeing a light at the end) is regarded by many as proof of their authenticity. The literature on this topic is growing rapidly (Sabom, 1982), and there are many believers.

Life after death is certainly an idea that many people, including me, wish to believe in. But reports of near-death experiences are not likely to convince anyone who does not passionately believe in life after death. There are, after all, alternative explanations for these experiences. For instance, the person may not have really been dead, in spite of the absence of vital signs. Or perhaps the experience was actually a dream the person had when he or she was regaining consciousness. And the commonality of the experiences had by many people could be a universal pattern of shutdown of the central nervous system. (For fuller scientific explanations see Abell and Singer, 1981.)

"The soul weighs 1/3000 of an ounce!" screamed the headline of the *Weekly World News* on November 1, 1988. From time to time we read in popular tabloids like this one that at the moment of death a person undergoes a minute loss of weight. This loss, some allege, signals the soul leaving the body and proves life after death.

Actually, this (weight-loss) claim is not well documented, but let's suppose, for the moment, that it is true. Is the soul's exit the only possible explanation for this loss? Even as nonscientists we could probably come up with some plausible alternatives. Perhaps it is a water loss due to evaporation. Or maybe when tissue dies, it undergoes a change in molecular structure that allows air molecules to enter and give a slight lift to the body.

When we are confronted with an extraordinary explanation of something, it is a good practice to ask ourselves this question: is this paranormal explanation the only possible one? For example, is life after death the only way to explain near-death experiences? Or is the soul the only way to explain a tiny weight loss at the moment of death?

Most of us would like to have proof of the existence of the soul or of life after death, so here's an area where we are prone to wishful thinking. But how can we tell when we are doing this? Is there a test we can give ourselves to detect our own wishful thinking? I believe there is—namely, asking two fruitful questions:

1. "Would I find this evidence compelling if I did *not* wish to believe what it supposedly proves?"
2. "Have I looked for other, ordinary explanations?"

A no answer to either of these questions suggests wishful thinking.

For example, if I accept an NDE as proof of life after death, I am probably indulging in wishful thinking because an NDE would not convert me if I disbelieved in life after death. (If evidence is really good, it turns doubters into believers.) And if I've made no effort to think of ordinary (and more probable) explanations for NDEs, this shows that I'm biased toward the paranormal explanation.

The *Loch Ness monster* is another idea that many people wish to believe. After all, there is a whole tradition (not to mention an industry) surrounding this notion. A frequently heard argument to support the monster's existence is that plesiosaurs (large, aquatic, prehistoric creatures) used to inhabit the area of Scotland around Loch Ness millions of years ago. Thus, it is possible that such a creature has survived in the loch, and this possibility has convinced many that the creature exists. Bad reasoning of this sort illustrates the *Fallacy of Deriving Fact from Possibility*. Its basic form is:

Premise: X is possible.
—————————————
Conclusion: Therefore, X is a fact.

Of course, we must admit that the stories about the monster could be true. But to say that the stories could be true does not provide the slightest reason to believe that they are true. A possibility is not evidence.

If the mere possibility of something were a good reason to believe it, there would be no limit to the number of things we should believe.

So, if we use this argument, we are probably succumbing to wishful thinking.

Perhaps the most blatant examples of wishful thinking are provided by people who embrace two opposing beliefs at the same time. This is extremely illogical thinking, but many (perhaps all) human beings are capable of it. This is called the *Fallacy of Doublethink,* and its basic form is:

> An idea is affirmed, but then another idea or act is expressed that is inconsistent with the first idea.

I am engaging in doublethinking if I believe that the world is going to end tomorrow but am planting trees in my yard today and look forward to seeing them bear fruit in five years. Thus, I believe that the world is going to end tomorrow *and* that the world is not going to end tomorrow. This, like all examples of doublethink, is believing a contradiction.

In 1986, on a San Diego television show, Penny Torres (the woman, mentioned above, who channels Mafu) was giving a demonstration. Some of the members of the audience were skeptical and expressed their doubts about the authenticity of what was going on. Then, one of Torres's devoted followers, in response to the attacks from the skeptics, said, "If I thought this was Penny Torres and not Mafu, I would still follow her anyway."

This person was saying that she could accept the idea that Torres was a fake. Yet at some deeper level she must have believed that this channeler was *not* a fake; otherwise, she wouldn't be willing to pay for her services. (Torres, at that time, was charging $200 for a private sitting and $500 for a weekend retreat.) The woman's need to believe in Mafu was evidently so strong that not even the knowledge that it was a sham could deter her.

Still another example of doublethink can be taken from the Reverend W. V. Grant's healing crusade. Grant uses a common trick employed by many faith healers: He asks people who have trouble walking to sit in a wheelchair during the crusade. Later, to give the illusion that miraculous healing has taken place, he has them rise out of their wheelchairs and walk around. The thousands of other people watching the show do not know that these people are quite capable of walking.

On the *West 57th Street* television show in 1987 a woman who had walked out of one of Grant's wheelchairs was asked if she had come in a wheelchair. "No," she said, "that was Rev. Grant's wheelchair. I don't own a wheelchair. But I feel much better." The reporter then asked her if she didn't think Grant's methods were questionable. "Well, I have to believe in a miracle anyway, because I prayed for this," she said.

The woman was aware that Grant was a trickster, but she also believed that he was a miracle worker! This was a good example of doublethink.

We See a Causal Connection Where None Exists   The Fallacy of False Cause, discussed in Chapter 3, illustrates the tendency that we have to infer a causal connection from a sequence of events. Here I'll mention two more fallacies in which causal connectedness is falsely ascribed.

The first is the *Fallacy of Explaining a Coincidence*. When an event is merely a coincidence, it needs no explanation. For example, if someone in your class on a particular day just happens to be wearing a shirt of the same color as yours, this is a coincidence. You would probably not attempt to explain it, because it needs no explanation: it happened merely by chance. An attempt to find an explanation for a correlation such as this is futile. The basic structure of this fallacy looks like this:

Premise: A and B occurred together.

Conclusion: Therefore, A and B were produced by the same cause.

When circumstances bring people and events together in a striking way, we often feel that it just couldn't be an accident, a coincidence. A friend of mine, while vacationing in Europe, saw a woman he had not seen since they were in the first grade together 25 years earlier in California. As it happened, they met in a London cathedral that they were both visiting because their other plans had fallen through that day. They spent some time together in London, decided to see each other after returning to the States, fell madly in love, and got married. He said to me: "Now, that just can't be a coincidence. There's just got to be a force guiding our lives."

But is there any reason to think that it was anything but a coincidence? Would this event persuade people who were not already inclined to believe in a "guiding force"? Or, better: would this event persuade people to believe in a guiding force who felt threatened by this idea because such a force would deprive them of their freedom? If my friend had cared to take the trouble, he could probably have discovered other spectacular coincidences taking place in that cathedral at the time. For example: two or more people who shared the same set of great-great-grandparents or two or more people who had studied flamenco guitar under the same instructor.

What makes some coincidences striking while others seem uninteresting is the significance that they do or do not have in our lives. Seeing someone wearing a shirt the same color as mine has no great impact on my life, but meeting a person from my hometown whom I later marry makes a world of difference in the course of my life. It is easy to understand, therefore, why some coincidences seize our attention and others are simply ignored.

A simple illustration of this tendency can be taken from a card game: If you were dealt all one suit in the game of bridge, you would be ecstatic, because this would be an instant winner. And when you calculated the probability of this happening, you might be converted to a belief in the supernatural. The chance of being dealt all clubs in bridge is one in 10 billion! But wait a minute. The chance of being dealt any other hand (even the useless ones) has exactly the same probability. So, the only reason to get excited about getting all clubs in bridge is because it is a winner. The fact that it happens only once in 10 billion hands is nothing to rave about, because this is true of every hand you're dealt in bridge.

The second fallacy in which causal connectedness is falsely ascribed is called *the Gambler;* its basic form looks like this:

Premise: A occurred.

Conclusion: Therefore, B has a high (or low) probability of occurring [when A has no influence on B].

Gamblers are frequently seduced into believing that random events influence one another. Here's an example: I was standing at a craps table at a casino in Lake Tahoe, Nevada, and a woman was rolling the dice. She seemed to be on a lucky streak, because she had rolled 7 (a winner) three times in a row. Just as she was starting to roll the dice again, my friend, a computer programmer and mathematician and a passionate gambler, placed his money on the "field." The field is every possible number that can show up on two dice except 7 and 11. She rolled a 4, and my friend, with a matter-of-fact air, picked up his winnings.

I was impressed, so I asked him how he had done it. He said he was making a very safe bet, because the probability that she would roll a 7 was extremely small after she had already rolled three of them.

He was committing the gambler's fallacy, because each roll of the dice (assuming that nothing is rigged) is completely independent of any other roll. The probability of a 7 turning up is always the same (one in six). His error was in thinking that her previous rolls would affect the latest one.

We Need Self-Respect   Self-respect, or self-esteem, is a basic need that we all have, and psychologists identify a wide variety of defense mechanisms that we employ to protect and preserve it. One such mechanism is called rationalization. We are rationalizing when we make up a story or excuse in order to avoid having to confront an ugly assault on our ego. For example, if I were not invited to a party that I had secretly been hoping to go to, I might say, "Oh well, I don't like parties anyway." If I can persuade myself of this, I have saved myself from a lot of hurt that could damage my self-image and diminish my self-esteem. Thus, defense mechanisms serve a useful psychological purpose, and we all make use of them from time to time.

Problems arise, however, if we use defense mechanisms too much or if we use them when we shouldn't. Examples of the latter tendency are easy to find among people who believe strongly in the paranormal.

In the Philippines (and elsewhere) *"psychic surgeons"* perform operations without knives. Thousands of patients travel to the Philippines each year for the procedure, which is a fraud done by simple sleight-of-hand techniques. During an "operation" blood appears, tissue is removed, and it looks as though the doctor's hands actually enter the body. When it's all over, however, there are no marks or scars, and the patient is politely told to leave.

On one occasion the "diseased tissue" that had supposedly been removed from the patient was recovered from the trash and found to be the blood and gizzard of a chicken. When this evidence was made public, some said that this only proved the doctor's extraordinary power: he had actually transformed a cancerous tumor into a chicken gizzard (Randi, 1980)!

When we bend over backward like this to explain away evidence that refutes what we believe, we are committing the *Fallacy of Rationalization*. The structure of this argument looks like this:

Premise: [A far-fetched idea is used to explain away data that disproves X.]

Conclusion: Therefore, X has not been disproved.

Because we can be very imaginative, we have almost unlimited power to deceive ourselves. Thus, we can preserve our belief in things that are bogus. Many people who believe in psychic surgery avoid legitimate treatment that could really help them. This is all too often a lethal mistake.

We can find another example of the fallacy of rationalization from the believers in Geller. Videotapes were made showing Geller using trickery to create the illusion of psychic power. When these tapes were shown to his fans, some said (rationalized) that he used cheating only when his psychic power had left him (Randi, 1975).

We Have Confidence in What We See   It is a sound principle that if you want to know something for sure, you've got to check it out for yourself. Firsthand experience is obviously better than hearsay evidence. As we say, seeing is believing.

But this piece of popular wisdom has made a great deal of fraud possible. One student said in class: "I know psychic surgery is real, because I saw it with my own eyes! I was standing just three feet away." He was obviously impressed with what he had seen, but if he had studied magic, he wouldn't have been. This student was committing the *Fallacy of Seeing Is Believing:*

Premise: I saw X with my own eyes [when I'm not a qualified observer].
_____

Conclusion: Therefore, X is real.

I've heard people say that they knew that Geller possessed psychic power because they themselves had seen him bend spoons with his mind. In fact, scientists themselves were convinced (before his fakery was exposed) by seeing him perform. It did not occur to them that being scientists did not qualify them as observers in this case. (See the earlier discussion of the Alpha Project.) Odd as it may seem, magicians are better observers than scientists when it comes to parapsychology.

We are right to have confidence in what we see, provided that we are qualified observers. When we draw conclusions about the reality of something that we are not qualified to judge, we are committing the fallacy of seeing is believing.

We Have Confidence in What We Feel   People sometimes experience a peculiar feeling or state of mind that convinces them that something paranormal has happened. Shirley MacLaine, for example, was sitting in a hot tub in Peru when she suddenly felt herself lifting out of her body and up through the roof and out to the moon and beyond the solar system to the remote stars and galaxies. "It wasn't my imagination; it was really happening!" (MacLaine, 1983).

There is no need to doubt that MacLaine's experience had a compelling quality, that is, that it really did seem as if she had left her body. (I, too, have had such experiences.) But does this mean that she really did leave her body? Clearly not. The fact that something *seems* real does not make it real. Making such an inference is committing the *Fallacy of Deriving "It Is" from "It Seems"*:

> Premise: X seems [or feels] real.
> _____
> Conclusion: Therefore, X is real.

When we look at the structure of this argument, we can see immediately that it is a non sequitur, that is, a fallacy. In order to establish that MacLaine was experiencing something real, that it was not just her imagination, we would need objective, empirical evidence. (For a discussion of how this might be done, see the Appendix, item 8.)

People who have a near-death experience are also prone to this fallacy. It does indeed seem to them that they had their experience while they were dead, but it does not follow that it actually happened then. Many of us have had the experience of taking a short nap and then waking up with the feeling that we have been asleep for several hours. Our waking impressions can be radically different from the actual facts. Similarly, though it may seem to people that their experience took place during the time they were dead, it doesn't mean that it really did.

Déjà vu is another experience that inclines some people to this fallacy: it *seems* as if I've been here before; therefore, I *have* been here before. But no matter how strong a "seeming" might be, it is no substitute for objective empirical evidence.

We Are Inconsistent Observers   We are continually forming theories and testing them by casual observation. I may suspect, for example, that people with brown eyes are never nearsighted. Every time I meet a brown-eyed person who is not nearsighted, I will count this as evidence for my theory. And if I meet a brown-eyed person who *is* nearsighted, I will have to give up my theory. But if I believe my theory passionately, I may tend to forget or simply ignore those cases that go against it. In order to discover the truth about this matter, I will have to recognize counterevidence should it occur. This means that I need to count all instances, whether they support my theory or not. If I notice the former and ignore the latter, I will get the impression that my theory is true even if it isn't. This tendency, unfortunately, is very common, and it is called the *Fallacy of Selective Perception:*

Premise: All observed cases of X have m [when the cases of X without m have been ignored].

Conclusion: Therefore, all cases of X have m.

"Every time Mike calls me on the phone, I know it's him before I pick up the receiver." People the world over have this experience and regard it as proof of extrasensory perception. And it *would* be proof if it actually did happen every time. (I am assuming that the phone calls don't fall into a time pattern that would make them predictable.)

Unfortunately, no attempt to verify ESP scientifically has ever produced solid evidence of it. But why do many conclude that they have ESP from the telephone experience? Part of the answer could be selective perception: they are *counting the hits and ignoring the misses.* They simply ignore the times when they thought it was Mike and it wasn't or the times when they thought it wasn't Mike and it was. If they kept careful records of their hunches, they would see that there were plenty of misses.

The myth about increased *crime (or accidents) on the night of a full moon* is kept alive in the same way. A student in my class testified that she worked in the emergency room at a hospital and had noticed an increase in accidents when there was a full moon. But these were casual observations. If she really wanted to find out whether there was a significant correlation between the moon and accidents (or crime), she would have to make consistent observations and keep careful records over a period of many months. Casual observations just aren't good enough.

Of course, there will be times when a full moon is accompanied by increased crime or accidents. But these must be weighed against the times when a full moon is *not* accompanied by increased crime or accidents. Serious investigations of this supposed correlation have been done, and the results have been entirely negative (Sanduleak, 1985).

We Are Prone to Interpretation   We are surrounded by a world of symbols, both spoken and written, and you are engaged in a symbolic activity at this moment as you read this. We have acquired the habit, through a lifetime of training and practice, of deciphering the meaning of symbols. If something is spoken or written, we naturally look for a message there. But herein lies a danger, because we may look for and "find" a message where there is none. This frequently happens in psychic readings.

When psychics do a reading on a person, they make many statements that are vague and general. Such statements have little or no empirical meaning (see Chapter 2), and they can easily be interpreted by the person to fit his or her particular case. Here are some examples:

> You are worried about something.
> Money is an important issue in your life.
> You like things to go your way.
> There is something you need to do.
> You've been going through some changes.
> You are about to make an important decision.
> You've had a serious handicap all of your life.

All of these statements can be interpreted as true by someone who wants to believe in the power of the reader. Take the last one: "You've had a serious handicap all of your life." When a student of mine was told this, she was very impressed with the reader's psychic powers, because she had been a diabetic since she was a child. But wait. Did the reader say that the student had diabetes? No, it was the *student* who said that. She projected a fact about herself onto the vague utterance of the psychic.

The student was committing the *Fallacy of Projected Specifics*. The structure looks like this:

Premise: So and so [whom I do not know] stated a specific fact about me [when so and so actually said something quite vague].
_____
Conclusion: Therefore, so and so has ESP.

This fallacy creates the illusion that an accurate message was conveyed by the reader's statement. But the reader did not even say that the handicap was a physical one or how serious the handicap was. Given this kind of latitude, it would be remarkable if the statement did *not* fit. It should be remembered, also, that many statements are made by the reader and that those that seem inaccurate are simply ignored (the fallacy of selective perception). They are not counted as misses indicative of the absence of psychic power. This means that the illusion of psychic power is practically guaranteed.

Another example of the fallacy of projected specifics can be found in the popular accounts of the prophecies of *Nostradamus*. Nostradamus was a 16th-century astrologer and physician who, it is said, accurately predicted the atomic bomb, air travel, submarines, Hitler, and the assassinations of John and Robert Kennedy. He even, it is said, spelled Hitler's name very nearly correctly: he said "Hister," which is off by only two letters. Of course, what the popular writers don't tell you is that *Hister* was the Latin name for the Danube and that Nostradamus is clearly referring to that famous river. In one place (Century V, verse 29) he even speaks of a bridge over Hister! (Hoebens, 1982).

For the most part the prophecies are extremely vague or obscure, and they lend themselves to just about any interpretation that looks good. For a long time many people thought that certain quatrains (the four-line verses in which Nostradamus wrote) had predicted Napoleon, but when Hitler came along, they changed their minds and decided that Nostradamus was talking about him instead. Here's an example of a quatrain (Century I, verse 60):

> An Emperor shall be born near Italy
> Who shall be sold to the Empire at a high price,
> They shall say, from the people he associates with,
> That he is less a prince than a butcher.

This quatrain has been interpreted variously as predicting Hitler, Napoleon, and Ferdinand II. All of them fit equally well, so which is it? Or try this one (Century I, verse 64):

> At night they will think they have seen the sun,
> When they see the half pig man:
> Noise, screams, battles seen fought in the skies:
> The brute beast will be heard to speak.

One popular writer, Erika Cheetham, interprets this quatrain as follows: The sun is a symbol of exploding bombs or searchlights, the half pig man is a pilot with goggles and oxygen mask, and the speaking beast refers to the use of radio (Cazeau, 1982). This is a superb example of the Fallacy of Projected Specifics.

We Are Often Naive   In my discussions with people about reports of paranormal happenings, I often hear, "But why would they [the people making the claim] lie to us?" A woman said this to me in March 1984 after hearing reports of poltergeist activity in Columbus, Ohio. (A poltergeist is defined as a noisy and mischievous ghost.)

Radio and television reporters said that telephones had mysteriously flown through the air, doors had sprung open, and lamps had tumbled to the floor in the home of Joan and John Resch. The odd thing was that these events occurred only when their 14-year-old daughter, Tina, was present. The hoax was revealed when a cameraman, who had come into the house to cover the story, left his video camera on (against Tina's instructions). The camera caught Tina in the act of pulling a lamp onto herself and screaming ("And a Child," 1984).

Why did Tina do it? I don't know, and you probably don't either, but it's important to know that she did do it. Hoaxes are far more common than most of us realize. (Remember Amityville? See Kurtz, 1986–1987.) It is simply naive to think that a paranormal story is true because we cannot imagine a motive for lying about it. When we do this, we are committing the *Egocentric Fallacy*. This fallacy consists of thinking that other people are just as honest as we are and that because we wouldn't deceive the public, no one else would. In argument form it looks like this:

Premise: I can think of no reason why so and so would want to deceive us.

Conclusion: Therefore, so and so is telling us the truth.

It's important, too, to remember that even when deliberate deception is not involved, it is wise to be skeptical. The person telling the story may be sincere and yet still be mistaken. Until evidence is exceedingly strong, the reports of a paranormal event should be regarded with suspicion.

Paranormal ideas are intriguing to think about and fun to talk about. But there are dangers, too. We need only recall the woman who froze to death in the wilderness in Minnesota while waiting to be picked up by a flying saucer (Frazier, 1983), the 900 people in Jonestown who killed themselves for a man whose divinity they were convinced of, or the thousands of people who suffer and die needlessly each year because of phony surgical operations. Naturally we want to keep an open mind, because some paranormal claims might turn out to be true. But let's keep a healthy skepticism in view of the fact that we are easily deceived and that there is no shortage of con artists out there eager to take advantage. A little skepticism could save our money, our lives, or both.

❏ Chapter Review Questions

1. Define the paranormal.
2. Why have paranormal phenomena not been accepted in mainstream science?
3. Why were the studies done on the paranormal at Duke University and Stanford Research Institute not accepted by mainstream science?
4. What was Project Alpha, and what did it accomplish?
5. What does CSICOP stand for?
6. What are the objectives of CSICOP?
7. What is a logical impossibility? Give an example.
8. Give an example of the Fallacy of Affirming a Logical Impossibility.
9. What is a physical impossibility? Give an example.
10. Who has the burden of proof, the believer or the skeptic, and why?
11. Why is it a fallacy to demand proof of a negative? Give an example of this fallacy.
12. What is Hume's scale, and what is it intended to accomplish?
13. What is the "popular philosophy"?
14. Does the "popular philosophy" offer good reasons for believing in paranormal phenomena?
15. How do the media contribute to belief in the paranormal? Give examples.
16. Explain how ignorance contributes to belief in the paranormal. Give examples.
17. What percentage of our brain do we actually use?
18. Is it true that people under hypnosis can't lie?
19. What is confabulation, and how does it relate to UFO abductions?
20. Explain how firewalking works.
21. Explain why dowsers are often successful at finding water.
22. Many ailments are self-curing. Why is this fact significant in a discussion of the paranormal?
23. What is the placebo effect?
24. How can precognitive dreams be explained scientifically?
25. What is cryptomnesia, and how does it relate to reincarnation?
26. Give an illustration of how scientific jargon can be used to impress someone who is ignorant of science.
27. What is the autokinetic effect, and what does it have to do with UFO sightings?
28. How has our growing scientific knowledge affected the number of "official" cures at Lourdes in France?

29. Explain the Fallacy of Jumping to Fantastic Conclusions. Give an example.
30. Give an example of how wishful thinking can distort a person's thinking about the paranormal.
31. How can you test yourself for wishful thinking?
32. Explain the Fallacy of Deriving Fact from Possibility. Give an example.
33. Explain the Fallacy of Doublethink. Give an example.
34. Why is it a fallacy to explain a coincidence? Give an example of this fallacy.
35. Explain the Fallacy of the Gambler. Give an example.
36. What psychological tendency gives rise to the fallacies of Explaining a Coincidence and the Gambler?
37. What is the Fallacy of Rationalization? Give an example.
38. What psychological tendency gives rise to the Fallacy of Rationalization?
39. Explain the Fallacy of Seeing Is Believing. Give an example.
40. Explain the Fallacy of Deriving "It Is" from "It Seems." Give an example.
41. Explain the Fallacy of Selective Perception. Give an example.
42. Explain the Fallacy of Projected Specifics. Give an example.
43. Explain the Egocentric Fallacy. Give an example.
44. What is the difference between the Fallacy of the Appeal to Ignorance (described in Chapter 3) and the Fallacy of Demanding Proof of a Negative?
45. What is the difference between the Fallacy of Seeing Is Believing and the Fallacy of Deriving "It Is" from "It Seems"?
46. Explain how skepticism can be beneficial.
47. Explain the difference between the False Cause Fallacy, the Fallacy of Explaining a Coincidence, and the Fallacy of the Gambler.

❏ Chapter Exercises

Use what you have learned from this chapter (and your own good sense) to critically analyze the following assertions. Suggested answers to exercises 1–10 are discussed in the back of the book.

1. Scientists don't believe in paranormal phenomena because they refuse to investigate them. If they would open their minds and simply look at the evidence, they would know.

2. Many scientists are skeptical of a paranormal claim because they cannot explain it. People are afraid of the unknown, and they refuse to acknowledge anything they cannot understand.

3. "My psychic power is still controversial; therefore, it's real" [Uri Geller, on *Magic or Miracle* TV show].

4. My power [to perform psychic surgery] is not mine. It's God's [the claim made by most psychic surgeons].

5. Everyone has psychic power. It's just that most of us don't realize it.

6. If a person goes to a quack and gets better, what's the harm in that?

7. Anything is possible.

8. You shouldn't be skeptical about levitation. After all, you don't know it's not real.

9. Past-life therapy is really effective for a lot of people. This means that reincarnation must be true. It's the only way to explain it.

10. One day, when playing cops and robbers, my friend fell, and (for a moment) it looked to me as if he had broken his left ankle. Actually he wasn't hurt at all, but six months later, he did fall and break that ankle, just as I had imagined it before. The bone was protruding out of the skin just as I had foreseen it. Now, how do you explain *that?*

11. You *can* get proof of astral travel, but you have to be open to it.

12. Skeptics have investigated all the UFO and abduction stories and found that none of them has substantial supporting evidence. But skeptics have still not proved that aliens from another world are not here.

13. If faith healers really had access to God's power, they could make a missing limb grow back instantly.

14. There's a woman in Charlotte, North Carolina, who says that she's seen the Jersey devil (which has a body and horns of an animal but the head of a man). I believe her, because she has no reason to make up such a story.

15. Members of the Lutz family admitted that the Amityville haunted house was a hoax. But how do we know that they weren't lying to us when they admitted it?

16. After I got home to my Chicago apartment, I lay down to rest. When I closed my eyes, I was instantly in London and it was foggy. I could literally smell the fog and feel it settling on my face. I could hear Big Ben sounding off four times, and I could see it faintly through the mist. It was amazing; I was really there!

17. You shouldn't be skeptical about ESP, because scientists have never proved that it doesn't exist.

18. UFOs have got to be real; there's just too much evidence. There have been thousands of sightings in all parts of the world, and now there are hundreds of people who tell about being kidnapped by extraterrestrials. The evidence is just too strong.

19. I'm pregnant, and there's a good chance it'll be a boy, because I've already had three girls.

20. The aliens won't let us discover them, because they don't want to cause a worldwide panic.

21. The reason that Inoko (a 17th-century Japanese samurai channeled by Marilyn Shultz) refuses to speak in Japanese is that he doesn't want English-speaking people to feel left out. That's a strict rule of etiquette from the Shogun period in Japan.

22. Astrology doesn't rule out free will. It's like turning the headlights on at night. It shows you what's up the road ahead so you can avoid that rock if you want to.

23. Ross: I'm going to try to park in the Main Street lot. This time I should be able to do it.

    Linda: That's crazy! We've tried six times before, and it's full every time. What makes you think you can do it this time?

    Ross: Well, if we've had six failures before, doesn't it seem likely that we'll succeed today?

24. Suppose we dug up 100 very specific predictions made 200 years ago by a psychic, and all had come true. This, certainly, would prove that precognition is real, wouldn't it?

25. Snodgrass: Mary is a Leo, and that explains why she is so friendly.

    Cuthbert: Oh come now, Snodgrass. That's astrology. It's bunk. Why do you believe in that stuff?

    Snodgrass: Do you deny that the sun, the moon, and the planets could have an influence on a person?

26. OK, I have no reason to think that bigfoot exists, but I also have no reason to think that bigfoot does *not* exist.

27. From the first day we moved into this house, the lights have gone dim (for a few seconds) for no apparent reason. Our neighbors have had no trouble with their electricity, so it's just our house. But we checked the wiring and found no problems at all. This shows that the house is definitely haunted.

28. "In 50 years we'll all be dead and gone, but psychic phenomena will continue because they exist" [Uri Geller, on the program *Is Anybody There?* 1989].

29. A neighbor told my mother that her [my mother's] baby would be born nine days early. And it was! Now, how do you explain that?

30. I saw Penny Torres channel Mafu, and I was very impressed. I'm an actor, and I can tell you, that was no act!

31. Rene DeHinden has had over 100 close encounters with UFOs, and he has taken numerous photographs of them. That's a lot of evidence, so UFOs must be real.

32. There have been sightings of bigfoot all over the world. Doesn't this prove that bigfoot exists?

33. I know crystals are useless, but I wear them anyway, just to be on the safe side.

34. When I channel dolphins, my body becomes as if it were one straight piece from the waist down, and my arms become flipper-like. It feels strange, but from this experience I've learned what it's like to be a dolphin.

35. I work in a carpeted department store, and today I noticed that the only people who did not get shocked from static electricity when they touched the metal frame of the display case were the ones who were friendly and smiled a lot.

36. Sometimes Chinese fortune cookies can be extremely accurate. In March I opened one that said I would soon be starting a long and difficult journey. Sure enough, in September I decided to become a lawyer and enrolled in a three-year law program.

CHAPTER 5

Science versus Pseudoscience

Skepticism is the chastity of the intellect.

George Santayana

In this chapter we will explore some of the reasons that the paranormal phenomena discussed in the previous chapter have not been given scientific validation. Millions of people not only embrace New Age beliefs but also think that they have proof for them. What is it about their method that falls short of legitimate science? Why are their beliefs called pseudoscience rather than real science?

❑ Characteristics of Science

We can answer these questions by first looking at 12 important characteristics of good science:

Science
1. It uses skepticism as an essential tool for gaining knowledge.
2. It combines an open mind with critical thinking.
3. It requires repeatability.
4. It requires testability.
5. It requires compatibility with existing knowledge.
6. It seeks out falsifying data.
7. It uses specific language.
8. It is empirical.
9. It does controlled experiments.
10. It guards against experimenter effects.

11. It is self-correcting.
12. It produces knowledge.

When our efforts to gain knowledge about the natural world proceed without these important features, we are doing pseudoscience. Thus, we can characterize pseudoscience as follows:

Pseudoscience
1. It has a negative attitude toward skepticism.
2. It equates an open mind with an uncritical one.
3. It does not require repeatability.
4. It is often not testable.
5. It is often incompatible with existing knowledge.
6. It explains away or ignores falsifying data.
7. It uses vague language.
8. It is not empirical.
9. It relies on anecdotal evidence.
10. It is vulnerable to experimenter effects.
11. It is not self-correcting.
12. It produces belief or faith but not knowledge.

In the bulk of this chapter I will illustrate these important differences with some examples.

Skepticism

In the fall of 1986 I attended a television show featuring people who claimed to be reincarnations of famous figures. One man said he was Napoleon. When questions were fielded from the audience, I explained that I had a friend who also believed that he was Napoleon and displayed quite a detailed knowledge of Napoleon's life. My question was: How can we tell which one (if either) is the real Napoleon?

The believers in the audience did not attempt to answer my question. Instead, they became irritated with me. They insisted that I was missing out on important spiritual growth by wasting my time doubting. They were clearly not troubled in the least by doubt, and they regarded my skepticism as a nuisance. Although they plainly enjoyed their belief, they were definitely not interested in knowing whether it was true.

This attitude toward skepticism was a certain indication that the discussion was not scientific, because science welcomes skepticism. Rather than shunning it, *science uses skepticism as an indispensable tool for gaining knowledge*. It is only by clearing away doubt that certainty can be approached. Without this process all we have is belief. The reason that science is so highly respected is that it is a rigorous method for gaining genuine knowledge, and at the core of this method is skepticism.

Linus Pauling and Vitamin C   It was skepticism that brought us closer to the truth about vitamin C and the common cold. Linus Pauling, one of the most highly respected scientists of our time, published several books praising the benefits of this nutrient. He asserted, among many other wonderful things, that large doses of vitamin C could prevent colds. But other scientists, after much careful testing and observing, failed to corroborate Pauling's claims (Marshall, 1986). On the other hand, if these tests had confirmed Pauling's claims, we would know that vitamin C did work to prevent colds.

Notice that the skepticism of science is not a respecter of persons. Pauling is a world-renowned scientist, and yet his claims for vitamin C were still rejected for scientific reasons. The fact that Pauling is a highly respected and capable scientist does not mean that he cannot make mistakes. This is yet another reason why genuine science gets and deserves our respect: truth is established not by authority but by evidence. In science Einstein's theory of relativity is regarded as true not because Einstein said it but because it has a great deal of supporting evidence. In the interest of seeking knowledge science applies a rigorous scrutiny to any and all claims, no matter who makes them. The strength and respectability of science is a direct result of this skepticism. (That science is highly respected is, ironically, demonstrated by the numerous pseudosciences that steal its name, for example, Scientology, scientific creationism, and the Unarius Academy of Science.

It's Common Sense   The skepticism of science is nothing new or special. It is actually just common sense. Skepticism is what we use whenever we really want to *know*. Suppose, for example, that you are shopping for a used car and the salesperson says, "This car is in perfect condition." Taking his word for it just won't be good enough. You're going to have to check it out for yourself (test it) if you really want to know what condition the car is in.

The same is true in science. When a provocative claim is made, scientists retain a skepticism that insists on proof by testing, experimenting, and observing. Nothing is considered known (proved) in science until it has been tested and retested many times and all significant doubts have been laid to rest. It is an unscientific attitude that rejects certain findings on the ground that the investigators are skeptical. This skepticism is a vital qualification for doing good science.

Open-Mindedness

People who are heavily into pseudoscience frequently accuse scientists of being closed minded. On more than one occasion I've heard something that sounds like this: "Scientists can't deal with anything that doesn't fit into their pre-established concepts. They won't even consider other possibilities." This is a very serious indictment if it's true. But is it?

Anyone who professes to be doing science must be open to new ideas, because *being open minded is vital to good science.* Our knowledge cannot progress if we don't consider new possibilities. We must remember that they laughed at Einstein, they laughed at Leonardo, and they laughed at Galileo. Many a great scientific advance has been initiated by a crazy-sounding idea.

On the other hand, we must remember that for every genius who was laughed at and was right, there were hundreds of crackpots who were laughed at and were wrong. History shows that the number of false ideas is vastly greater than the number of true ones, and scientific progress would be much slower than it is if scientists were not discriminating. All ideas are not of equal value; some are much better than others. Much time and energy would be wasted if scientists investigated every idea, no matter how bizarre. And remember, science *has* investigated many paranormal claims and has failed to get positive results. Perhaps this is the reason that many scientists are impatient and even seem closed minded regarding these claims.

When I, as a skeptic, challenge the claims of New Age people, I am frequently accused of being closed minded. This is absurd thinking, because it defines an open mind as one that asks no questions and has no doubts. It equates an open mind with a blank mind. But if we are interested in knowledge, we must have both an open mind and a critical one. We have no choice about this. In order to separate the true from the false, we must press our skeptical questions to the limit. *The quest for knowledge requires critical thinking.*

Repeatability

I've often heard people say something like this: "One day, when coming home from school, I had a clairvoyant experience. I imagined my grandmother being taken to the hospital, and when I got home, my mother told me it was actually true. My grandmother was having a heart attack, and she was in intensive care. That was real ESP, but it's only happened to me once in my life." This is an interesting story, but from a scientific point of view it is not evidence of ESP, because it happened only once. Was it really ESP or just a coincidence?

It is a fundamental principle of science that if a phenomenon occurs once, it will occur again, if the conditions are the same. Thus it is possible for one scientist to test the claim of another scientist by copying the procedure to see whether the result is the same. This is called a *replication study*. Replication studies are required in science, because it is all too common for scientists to think that they've discovered something when they haven't. This happens to scientists and nonscientists alike. If one scientist claims to have proved ESP in the laboratory using a certain gifted individual, other scientists should be able to get the same results using this same person under identical conditions.

In the previous chapter I mentioned that replication failures are the reason that ESP has not been accepted as real by the scientific community. The belief that a full moon causes an increase in crime has been rejected for the same reason (Sanduleak, 1985). It often happens that when a claim is made, research is cited to back it up. Both ESP and the moon-crime connection have been supported by studies that were supposedly legitimate, but those studies have been superseded by later studies. We can, however, still find recent literature in abundance that neglects to mention replication failures and cites discredited studies as proof. *It is a common characteristic of pseudoscience that data known to be invalid are still used as evidence.*

Scientific knowledge is not always easy or quick, and one or two studies are not always enough. All claims must be validated by numerous replication studies before they can be called true. So, when we hear about an exciting discovery—for example, that scientists have discovered how to get cheap, safe energy from "cold fusion"—our response should be: "That's great if it's true. Now let's wait and see what replication studies show." In other words, we should never be too quick to accept anything as scientifically proved. This would not be good scientific thinking.

Testability

One evening in the spring of 1987 I attended a class in parapsychology in which the instructor was preparing to give a demonstration of table tipping. The instructor and four or five students sat around a small, lightweight, wicker table with their hands resting on the edges. The students were encouraged to ask questions of spirit guides who were supposed to exist in another dimension. The table was supposed to tip in response to the question. One tip meant no, two meant yes. To spell out a word, one tip meant "A," two "B," and three "C."

Many questions were asked, and the table gave many answers—it was extremely obliging. The students were very impressed, and, in fact, one student had to leave the table because she was trembling so badly. She had been terrified by the experience of communicating with a brother who had been dead for six months.

After the demonstration the instructor had some interesting things to say:

1. Black repels negative energy. (So, we keep the table covered with a black cloth when it is not in use.)
2. Each person has seven spirit-entity guides, one chief guide and six others.
3. Some spirit entities are insane, but most are normal.
4. Everyone has an aura of psychic energy.
5. We choose our own incarnations.
6. Spirit entities from the fourth, fifth, sixth, and seventh dimensions communicate to us telepathically and use the auric energy field to move the table.

As the instructor spoke, I got the feeling that I had entered a metaphysical no-man's-land in which anything goes. It seemed as if we were playing a game of words without any rules. She could say anything at all, and we were supposed to accept it. And it was apparent that most of the people there *were* accepting everything she was saying.

Clearly, we can believe anything we want, but if we are to go beyond belief to knowledge, we will need to test and confirm these claims. But how could this be done? What observations could we make that would show any of them to be true or false? Take point 2, for instance. I might sit at the table while it's tipping and have some intriguing experiences. (And I probably will, because the instructor has planted suggestions: "You might feel a tingling in your hands, or you might feel heat. You might feel just anything while you're at the table.") I may even have experiences that convince me that I have seven spirit-entity guides. But this is only a "seeming." I still need to know whether what seems real actually is real. (Recall the fallacy of deriving "it is" from "it seems.") Beyond my own subjective experiences that my imagination and believing mind might interpret as the real thing, there seems to be no way of testing these experiences.

In order to be called scientific, an idea must be testable. In other words, it must be possible to make observations that provide evidence for or against the idea. Some ideas are directly testable, such as the idea that it is raining outside. To test this we need only look out the window. But most of the ideas that science deals with are testable only indirectly.

Legionnaires' Disease   Take, for example, the idea that Legionnaires' disease was caused by food poisoning. At an American Legion convention in Philadelphia many conventioners fell ill, and some died. The U.S. Centers for Disease Control (CDC) thought that hotel food might have been responsible. This is a scientific hypothesis (idea), because we can make certain observations that would confirm or disconfirm it.

What observations? Well, if it was the food, we can predict that all the victims must have eaten the same food. This is an observable consequence of the hypothesis that food caused the problem. When we can deduce observable consequences from an idea in this way, it is said to have *predictive power*. So, given the hypothesis:

Food poisoning made the Legionnaires sick,

we can make the prediction:

All the sick Legionnaires ate the same food

as an observable consequence. As it happened, the CDC investigated and found that they had not all eaten the same food; hence, the hypothesis was rejected.

Having disposed of the food-poisoning hypothesis, the CDC went on to try, and eliminate, several others. Was it a virus? No. Was it a toxic chemical? No. Ultimately the CDC discovered that the cause was a pernicious bacterium. It reasoned:

Hypothesis: A pernicious bacterium made the Legionnaires sick.
Prediction: We should find the same bacterium in the blood of
              all the victims.

Blood samples from all the victims showed that the bacterium was indeed the (probable) cause of the disease.

Evolution   Another example of a good scientific hypothesis is the theory of evolution. This idea has enormous predictive power and testability:

> Hypothesis: Present-day life forms evolved over vast stretches of time from simpler forms.
>
> Predictions: 1. In the fossil record we should find the simplest life forms in the earliest geological strata and progressively more complex life forms in the more recent geological strata.
> 2. We should *not* find a fossil of a vertebrate in the oldest strata containing the earliest life forms.
> 3. We should find fossilized or living transitional forms between invertebrates and vertebrates.
> 4. We should find fossilized or living transitional forms between reptiles and mammals.

These are only some of the predictions that can be deduced from the theory of evolution. They are empirical consequences of this idea, and the fact that they have been abundantly observed is the reason that scientists consider evolution well established.

Everyday Scientific Reasoning   This form of reasoning is not unique to science. In fact, *we use scientific reasoning every day*. Here's an example: "Is the car battery dead?" "I don't know. Try the lights."

> Hypothesis: The battery is dead.
> Prediction: The lights won't turn on.

We predict that if the battery is dead, the lights will not come on, and we test the hypothesis by observing a predicted consequence of it. If the lights do come on, we've refuted (falsified) the hypothesis that the battery is dead. If the lights do not come on, we have some (but not conclusive) evidence that the battery is dead. If we check the wiring, the lightbulbs, and the connections and they are working, we can safely conclude that the battery is indeed dead.

Now glance back briefly at the statements made by the parapsychology instructor. Do any of them have any predictive power and testability? In other words, can we deduce observable consequences from any of them? Let's try point 5:

We choose our own incarnations.

Can we deduce from this hypothesis that if you ask people whether they chose their present incarnation, they will say yes? No, because the hypothesis does not say or imply that you must remember having chosen your present incarnation. Observing that people say yes in response to this question would not support the hypothesis. Could any other observations support the hypothesis? It seems not.

Well, can we deduce observable consequences that would refute it? Can we say, for example, that the hypothesis is false if people answer no when asked the same question? It seems not, because forgetting the act of having chosen your incarnation could simply be an aspect of the chosen incarnation. What about the fact that some people are born hopelessly retarded and deformed; and what about the fact that some children have sadistically abusive parents? Do these observations count against the claim? In discussions with believers on this question, I have been told that a person might choose such an incarnation as a form of penance for wrongs committed in a past life. Try as we might, the hypothesis seems to be totally unverifiable and totally unfalsifiable. It is, therefore, *not testable and not scientific.* (It also lacks empirical meaning; see Chapter 2.)

Testing a Channeler   Many people claiming psychic powers flatly refuse to be tested. Penny Torres, mentioned in the previous chapter, is a housewife from Los Angeles who has recently achieved fame and fortune as a channeler for Mafu, a spirit being whose last physical embodiment supposedly occurred in Pompeii in the first century. Torres was invited to give a demonstration on the *Stanley Tonight* television show in San Diego, and I was invited to attend.

While Torres was in a channeling state, that is, while Mafu was speaking, people from the audience were encouraged to ask questions. Some typical questions were: "Why are children today so rebellious?" "Why have you come here?" "What is your message to us?" "What does it mean to live in the present?" These questions, as you can see, were vague and general, and Mafu was happy to supply vague and general responses to them.

Throughout our session with Mafu we were repeatedly told that we were loved by God the Father and that He wanted us to love ourselves. This may be an important message and, psychologically, a very beneficial one, but it is hardly new. Except for a small handful of skeptics in the audience, everyone seemed pleased with the revelations coming forth. But it should have occurred to anyone with a modicum of critical distance that none of them constituted evidence of authenticity.

I attempted to change that. When the microphone came to me, I asked: "Quogare ibetos mongallum durandis?" (This was just nonsense that I created to sound like Latin.) She (he) responded: "You ask me to speak in another language. Entity, listen to magnetic recordings if you want to hear other languages." Then I said, "You may answer in English," and she (he) responded: "I will not placate your tests. So be it." (This was a curious response, because at the begining of the show she told us that she and Mafu had been tested by a scientist.)

Torres's response was unfortunate, because testing is the only way in which we can go beyond a parlor game to something really significant. In other words, it's the only way in which we can go beyond belief to knowledge. If the channeler had demonstrated a command of ancient Latin without ever having studied it, that would have been significant evidence. If she had told us something new about Pompeii that could be verified and proved enlightening to historians, that, too, would have been significant evidence. But instead, all we got were vague generalities and comforting platitudes that we had heard many times before. That, of course, was quite enough for her many followers, who were much more interested in believing than in knowing.

After the taping of the show Torres left the studio in a long, white limousine.

Compatibility

A man claiming to be psychic, whom I invited to my class, said he had X-ray vision and that he practiced psychic surgery. He went on to explain that psychic surgery was a process made possible by a form of energy that traveled faster than the speed of light. Now, this is a very intriguing idea, especially since Einstein said that nothing could travel faster than the speed of light. But, of course, Einstein could be wrong. It's not the fact that he said it that's important but the fact that numerous tests and observations have consistently confirmed what he said. The psychic's claim should give us pause, because it is incompatible with a hypothesis that is well supported by evidence. Of course, it is not logically impossible for the psychic to be right, but he had better have extremely good evidence; otherwise, giving him serious consideration is not warranted.

A good scientific hypothesis must be compatible with other hypotheses that have already been well confirmed. In other words, there should not be a conflict with what is known. If the truth of the proposed idea would require a rejection of other well-established ones, the idea lacks compatibility. A good example is the idea that the universe is only 6,000 years old. (This figure is derived by totaling the generations listed in the Bible from Adam and Eve through Abraham to the present day.)

The universe is only 6,000 years old.

If we are to seriously entertain this hypothesis, we will have to make drastic revisions of many branches of science, for example, astronomy. The science of astronomy has calculated the distance to the nearest galaxies to be 2.5 million light-years, and the most distant objects we observe (quasars) are over 10 billion light-years away. (A light-year is the distance that light travels in one year, or 6 trillion miles.) This means that those objects we observe with our telescopes are millions or billions of years old, since it took that long for their light to travel through space to reach us. And what about geology? How long, according to geologists, did it take to form the Grand Canyon? Millions of years. And what about physics and chemistry? How long does it take to form Pb-207? This is one of the isotopes of lead that is a decay product of U-235, one of the isotopes of uranium. This decay process is very slow, because the half-life of U-235 is 713 million years. This means a chunk of pure U-235 would be half lead in 713 million years. The samples of Pb-207 that we can observe, then, are extremely old, much older than 6,000 years.

Clearly, if we are to take seriously the idea that the universe is 6,000 years old, we will have to either drastically revise or simply discard most of established science. The evidence for this hypothesis would have to be extraordinary to justify such radical measures. But in the absence of such evidence, the hypothesis must be rejected on the ground of its gross incompatibility with the existing and well-established framework.

Falsifiability

Parapsychology is notorious for its excuses for failed experiments. J. B. Rhine, of Duke University, invented the term *psi-missing* to refer to ESP tests in which his subjects scored below chance level (Hansel, 1985). Such performances, Rhine reasoned, must be indications that psychic energy was interfering with the subject's attempt to hit the target. How's that for logic? If you win, you win; and if you lose, you win. A low score on a test does not indicate the absence of psychic forces; it confirms it! Using maneuvers like this makes Rhine's position unfalsifiable and, therefore, empirically meaningless (recall from Chapter 2) and unscientific.

When skeptics were unable to replicate Rhine's successful experiments, he attributed their failure to the fact that the experimenters were skeptics. He contended that the presence of skeptics had affected the subjects and destroyed their ESP power. Here, again, the parapsychologist did not let the failure count against ESP. Because he refused to allow falsifiability, what Rhine was doing in the laboratory was not science but pseudoscience.

Another example of a maneuver to avoid falsifiability is the "shyness effect." This is a term coined by John Taylor of the University of London, who tested many children for psychokinesis. He noticed that the children could not perform when they were supervised, but when they were not supervised, they could perform beautifully. This did not, according to Taylor, count against psychokinesis, it only showed that psychokinetic power did not like to be observed! Later, a hidden video camera proved that the children were cheating, and Taylor changed his position on psychokinesis to "unproved" (Kurtz, 1986).

To these historical cases of how pseudoscientists avoid falsifiability, I can add a personal experience of my own. In the spring of 1987 I invited a psychic into my classroom to give "cold readings." In a cold reading the psychic addresses a person at random and states facts about him or her. This display is supposed to demonstrate paranormal powers, because the reader has never seen the person before. Our psychic looked at a student in the front row, and in the dialogue that followed she showed great skill in avoiding disproof.

Psychic: You are a musician.

Student: No.

Psychic: You *like* music [rephrasing].

Student: No.

Psychic: Someone close to you is a musician [enlarging the target].

Student: No.

Psychic: You may have repressed your interest in music [psychologizing].

Student: [no response]

Psychic: In a group this large you get interference. That is, I may think I'm picking up information about a particular person when in fact I'm really picking up information about someone else in the room [changing targets].

Student: [no response]

Psychic: You like things to go your way [ignoring: since we're not getting anywhere with music, let's try another topic].

This psychic used five different tactics for evading or explaining away falsification. How many are possible? It seems that there can be as many as the imagination permits. But this sort of maneuvering (recall from Chapter 2) makes the reader's pronouncements empirically meaningless and, therefore, unscientific. It is an exercise in self-deception, and it is a common characteristic of pseudoscience.

By contrast, *all scientific claims must be falsifiable, and good scientific technique often consists of seeking out falsifying data.* If an idea is true, a search for falsifying data will be fruitless. Should this happen, it is strong evidence for the idea. Take, for example, the idea that hibernation in bears is triggered by subzero temperatures. A good way to confirm this theory would be to try to make a bear go into hibernation by varying other factors in temperatures above zero. If we try, and fail, to induce hibernation by reducing the bear's food, sunlight, and sexual activity, we have strong evidence to support the hypothesis.

Or take this example: If we believe that all swans are white, a good way to confirm this idea would be to look everywhere for a black (or other nonwhite) swan. If we can't find one, we have good reason to believe that all swans are white. For many years English and American biologists believed that all swans really were white, because they had never seen any other kind. The hypothesis later had to be rejected when, in Australia, a species of black swan was discovered.

Language: Specific versus Vague

Vague language is common in pseudoscience, and it is the stock-in-trade of psychic readers. There are two obvious advantages to the use of vague language:

1. Listeners can interpret what is said in any way they like, creating the illusion of an accurate reading.
2. The risk of falsification is greatly reduced, making it unnecessary to employ the evasive tactics mentioned above.

But it is this vagueness that makes the reader's statements empirically meaningless and, consequently, unscientific. Take, for example, the frequently used pronouncement "You are planning to make a change." Because no specific change is mentioned, listeners can interpret it to fit their case, no matter what it is. (Recall the Fallacy of Projected Specifics in Chapter 4.) "Make a change" could apply to jobs, careers, friends, houses, vacations, or even brands of toothpaste. Moreover, because the application is so broad, it is difficult to imagine whom it could *not* apply to (unfalsifiable).

From a scientific point of view such a vague statement is useless, because it is not clear what observations would tend to confirm or disconfirm it. In other words, it is not testable. *To be scientifically acceptable, a statement must be specific in order to be testable.* For contrast, let's consider the statement "Jim is planning to move from California to Idaho." This statement is testable because it is specific: we can make observations to confirm or disconfirm it. In making these observations, we are using the scientific method whether we are scientists or not.

For example, if we find that Jim has gone to interview for jobs in Idaho, has told his neighbors that he is moving to Idaho, has made a deposit on an apartment in Idaho, and has given notice to his landlord and to his boss at work, we have very strong evidence that he is planning a move to Idaho. On the other hand, if we find that he has just purchased a home in Pasadena, has just joined the Pasadena Country Club, and is looking for a new job in Los Angeles, we have strong evidence that he is not planning a move to Idaho.

Now, if the reader had said something as specific as this, her statement would be scientifically respectable, because it would be testable. And if she turned out to be correct, this result would be highly significant. Assuming that she did not use ordinary means of obtaining the information and assuming that her performance was repeatable, it could mean that she actually had extrasensory powers. But this, of course, is not what happens.

Method of Investigating: Empirical versus Nonempirical

Occult and pseudoscientific literature is replete with personal accounts. Many people (this writer included) have had out-of-body experiences or the experience of apparently reading someone's mind. In almost every class I teach there is at least one person who has had the experience of dowsing for water. "I could hardly keep the stick in my hands because the force pulling it down was so strong," said one student. Another student told us about the experiences (dreams, sensations, thoughts) that she had had while she was clinically dead.

Such testimony seems compelling, and it's not reasonable to deny that people do have such experiences. But if they are real experiences, why are they not accepted as scientific proof? The answer to this question is that these experiences do not constitute empirical evidence of the kind required by science. To the dowser it may, indeed, feel as though the stick is being pulled down by a strong force. But science requires a public demonstration that the stick can actually be used to find water, and this has never been done. The dowser's subjective experience of the force pulling on the stick could easily be his or her imagination.

Pseudoproof and Real Proof   Many of the experiences of paranormal phenomena that people report can be explained in terms of two factors: belief and imagination. It is important to realize the power of this formula:

> Belief + Imagination = "Proof"

If you've been told that a spirit being from the seventh dimension is going to visit you, you need only believe this and your imagination will do the rest. If you truly believe that dowsing works, it will really seem as if there is a force tugging on the stick. And if you truly believe in spiritualism, you will easily feel a ghostly hand touching you on the shoulder in a seance (Kane, 1985).

So, although the field of the paranormal boasts innumerable accounts of experiences, many of them are not experiences of the kind required by science. *In science, the test of truth is the evidence presented to the five senses from the public arena.* If a phenomenon is real, it can be witnessed by all who are present, believers and skeptics alike. But when scientists carefully test and observe a dowser, they do not see him finding the pipe with water in it. When scientists carefully test and observe a telepathist, they do not see her hitting the target image. (Actually, the dowser and the telepathist are sometimes correct, but the number of hits does not exceed chance expectations.) And, though some people report feeling the hand of a ghost on their shoulder, scientific observers do not see the ghost.

Reality of the Unseen   Some people think that because science is empirical, it does not believe in anything we cannot see, touch, smell, taste, or hear. This is simply not true. Particle physicists of today are concerned almost exclusively with radiations they cannot see, forces they cannot feel, and bits of matter they cannot touch. But all of the hypotheses concerning these phenomena must have predictive power and be testable. Any notion that is scientific must lead us ultimately to observable entities such as rocks, clocks, pointer readings, and lines on photographic plates. There must be the possibility of making public observations that would tend to confirm or disconfirm the hypothesis.

Controlled Studies versus Anecdotal Evidence

If you walk into almost any bookstore, you can find many books written about the power of crystals to heal people. This literature is filled with accounts of people who used these stones to cure an ailment, to acquire a new power, or to enhance an old one. It's fun to read these stories; they're about real people with real experiences, and for this reason they seem quite believable.

Stories about real people are even more interesting and believable when they are told by the people themselves. For this reason television and radio talk shows frequently make use of guests who tell their personal experiences confirming astrology, crystals, or ESP on the air. This is a technique that would not be used if it didn't have great audience appeal. Anecdotal evidence (stories), especially in large quantities, often impress and persuade.

But *stories, even true ones, do not constitute scientific evidence*. The tendency of people to be misled by success stories is so common that it deserves a special name. Let's call it the Fallacy of Positive Cases:

Premise: Several cases show that X is effective [when the failures have not been sought out].

Conclusion: Therefore, X is effective.

This fallacy is committed when we are impressed by confirmatory reports and do not inquire about disconfirmatory ones. We are easily impressed by success stories, but the number of successes is meaningless unless we know the number of failures. *It is not the number of successes that is important but the ratio of the successes to the failures*. We may hear of hundreds who wore crystals and cured their hives, but this means nothing if there were millions who tried them and failed. Many times we do not hear about the failures because people are embarrassed that they wasted time and money or because they have simply forgotten. A treatment is newsworthy only if it works, or seems to.

Personal Experience   Anecdotal evidence always concerns someone's personal experience, and the person who had the experience is usually totally convinced. "I tried starch blockers and lost weight," said a friend of mine. "I know they work." The starch blocker was a new diet aid that (it was said) allowed you to eat as much carbohydrate food as you liked and still lose weight, because the assimilation of carbohydrates into the body was inhibited. My friend (as well as many others) was drawn irresistibly to the conclusion the starch-blocker pills caused him to lose weight.

But this is too hasty. It is, in fact, the False-Cause Fallacy again (see Chapter 3). How does he know that he wouldn't have lost weight without those pills? In his isolated case he does not know what the relevant factors were, because *any particular effect can have any number of causes.* Without a controlled experiment he simply cannot know that the treatment caused the loss of weight.

Controlled Studies   In order to find out whether starch-blocker pills actually cause weight reduction, a controlled study needs to be done. When possible, *good science requires controlled studies.* In a controlled study of starch blockers two groups are formed, both made up of overweight people. The groups are made equal in every possible respect that is relevant: health history, diet, rest, exercise, and so on. Even the pills administered to each group are identical in appearance, size, weight, and taste. The only difference between the two groups is that one of them gets the real starch-blocker pill, and the other gets a fake, or placebo. The first group is called the *experimental group,* and the second group is called the *control group.* The control group, or placebo group, is necessary for comparison in order to see what difference the starch blockers make.

This setup is also called a *blind experiment,* because the subjects do not know whether they are taking an active substance. To make the test even more objective, it is performed in a *double-blind* fashion: this means that neither the people taking the pills nor the experimenters know which people are getting the starch blockers and which are getting the placebos. Each subject in the experiment is assigned to a group by computer. During the experiment only the computer knows whether a person is an experimental subject or a control subject.

At the end of an established period the change in weight of each subject is measured and recorded. The computer code is then broken, and the data from the two groups are compared. If the experimental group has lost more weight than the control group, this is strong evidence that starch blockers actually cause weight reduction. If there is no difference in the weight fluctuations of the two groups, we can say that starch blockers do not cause weight reduction. If the experimental group has gained weight but the control group has not, it is a rude surprise showing that starch blockers actually make you gain weight!

As it happens, the controlled studies that have been done show starch blockers to have no effect on body weight. But this result could not really be known until a controlled study was performed. Starch blockers are still sold over the counter in some places in spite of a ban by the U.S. Food and Drug Administration.

How a Quack Quacks Quack medicine in the United States alone is a $10-billion-a-year industry (*NCAHF Newsletter,* 1987). Every remedy, no matter how useless, has plenty of success stories to go with it. We should, therefore, learn to keep a cool head when we hear rave reports about a new medical wonder. The person who does not think critically is extremely easy prey, because a quack doctor always seems to have an adequate response, regardless of the outcome of the treatment:

1. The patient gets better.
   Response: "The treatment was a success."
2. The patient stays the same.
   Response: "The treatment has had a stabilizing effect, and the cure will take more time."
3. The patient gets worse.
   Response: "We need to increase the dose."
4. The patient dies.
   Response: "The treatment was delayed too long."

The way to bypass this chicanery and get to the truth is to ask if there were controlled studies. Without these, the treatment does not have scientific backing, and you fly at your own risk.

Experimenter Effects

Classes in parapsychology are becoming very popular, and experiments are being performed in them that apparently demonstrate ESP. In one telepathy experiment I witnessed, the sender concentrated her attention on a picture while the receiver made marks, drew pictures, and wrote words on a blank piece of paper to record her impression of the telepathic transmission.

After five minutes had passed, the receiver's paper was compared with the target picture. The target picture was an aerial view of a red car passing swifly over a wet street. White sprays of water fanned out from both front wheels. The receiver had drawn many shapes (triangles, rectangles, squares), drawn many lines (straight, curved, broken), and written many words (*red? anger? white? fluffy, happy, light, soar, kind? swim? high, sly*). The instructor said this was an accurate reading, because the word *red* was a hit, the words *white* and *fluffy* fit the sprays of water, and the curved line resembled the contours of the car's body.

Testing ESP Pseudoscientifically From a scientific (and common-sense) standpoint this experiment is absurd for at least three reasons. First, the items that do not fit are ignored and not counted against the accuracy of the reading (the Fallacy of Selective Perception). Second, the chance that the receiver will get a few hits is extremely high because of the large number of items she put on her paper. This is the *shotgun effect*: the more bullets you fire, the better your chance of hitting something. Similarly, the more predictions you make, the greater the chance that one of them will come true.

The shotgun effect explains why many psychics have a few successful predictions to boast of. But of the numerous predictions made by psychics, we hear only about the ones that come true; we don't hear about the greater number that don't come true. For example, it is not well known that the famous psychic Edgar Cayce predicted that China would become Christian in 1966. Jeanne Dixon is another example: most people have heard that she predicted the assassination of John F. Kennedy (actually, she did no such thing), but few people know that she predicted that Kennedy would *not* be elected president (Cazeau, 1982).

A third reason that the classroom experiment is absurd is that it is prone to *experimenter effects*. Experimenter effects occur whenever the experimenter influences, in any way, the apparent results of the test. In the present experimental setup there are no rules stating whether something is a hit or not. Does the word *fluffy*, for example, really fit the water sprays? This is purely a matter of interpretation. And what about that curved line drawn by the receiver? Does it really fit the profile of the car in the photo? Clearly, these correspondences are entirely in the eye of the experimenter.

Testing ESP Scientifically   A properly designed experiment in mental telepathy would use a finite set of unambiguous pictures in order to avoid the problem of biased interpretation from the experimenter. *Good scientific experiments are designed to guard against experimenter effects.* Such tests have been performed using Zener cards. One of five possible pictures appears on each card: a square, a circle, a star, wavy lines, and a cross. There are 5 cards bearing each picture, making a deck of 25 cards. Of course, tests with these cards do not preclude the possibility of cheating, but they at least remove the element of experimenter interpretation. Carefully designed tests using these cards have not produced any solid evidence of ESP.

Animal Language   Another example of research that is prone to experimenter effects is the work being done with animal language. Researchers report having taught apes to communicate using American Sign Language. But whether a particular gesture or movement made by the ape is actually a word or sentence seems to be a matter of experimenter interpretation. There are no clear rules for distinguishing correct from incorrect signing in apes. Consequently, ambiguous signing frequently counts as correct, and many odd combinations of signs (for example, when the verb precedes the subject) are shrugged off as "chimp accent" (*Laser,* April–June, 1987).

In Germany, around the turn of the century, a horse gained notoriety through its apparent ability to calculate. When asked a question of arithmetic, Hans could tap out the answer with his hoof. If a perfect stranger asked him for the square root of 16, Hans would promptly come back with four taps. This case seemed to indicate that animals were far more intelligent than ever thought.

But psychologists became a bit skeptical when they discovered that if the person asking the question didn't know the answer, Hans didn't either. Careful observing and testing revealed the horse had a remarkable ability to pick up body-language cues from people. By monitoring subtle changes in their posture, breathing, and facial expressions, Hans could determine when to stop tapping. This phenomenon has been dubbed the "Clever Hans Effect." It occurs whenever the experimenter unconsciously cues the subject to give the right answer. It is a serious example of an experimenter effect, and it has been a constant flaw in animal language research.

Self-Correction

The history of science is replete with examples of new knowledge replacing old. A few that come immediately to mind are the flat earth, the geocentric model of the universe, spontaneous generation, "flogiston," ether-filled space, the Piltdown hoax, and the belief that vitamin C prevents colds. All of these ideas were at one time embraced by scientists, and it was the growth of scientific knowledge that exposed them as false. That scientific opinion changes is not a weakness but a strength. It means that *science is a self-correcting process* that ferrets out its own errors and brings us ever closer to the truth.

Similar examples are conspicuously absent in the pseudosciences. We do not find, for example, a discovery in astrology that made astrologers revise or reject the old principles. The practice of astrology has not undergone any changes, as a result of discoveries, in the 2,000 years of its existence. We do not find parapsychologists making discoveries about mental telepathy that cause them to revise or reject their previous assumptions about ESP. And we do not hear about discoveries that make believers in channeling admit that their previous ideas were wrong. Unlike science, *pseudoscience is not self-correcting*.

Knowledge versus Belief

That pseudoscience is not self-correcting stems directly from the abandonment of an objective method that would permit both confirmation and disconfirmation of its claims. Its claims turn out to be nothing more than expressions of attitudes rather than empirically meaningful assertions (see Chapter 2). The price it pays is that its own errors are never recognized and real progress is never made. It can, and does, create belief or faith, but it can never make legitimate claims to knowledge.

We have the right and the freedom to believe whatever we want, but there is a vast difference between believing and knowing. To know that something is true is to be able to answer adequately the question "How do you know?" In other words, we can give empirical (testable) reasons for asserting our claim. If we can't give such reasons, our "knowing" is actually nothing but believing in disguise.

When we do science, we are employing a method of making sure, of knowing. Observing and testing are simply the best ways we have of determining whether an idea is really true. When an idea has been tested and confirmed many times, we have the credentials for saying that we know it to be true. *It is only by doing science that we can go beyond belief to genuine knowledge.*

❑ Words of Caution about Science

Science Deals in Probabilities

All of the pronouncements of science are based on empirical evidence. So, the stronger the evidence for a claim, the greater our confidence in it. An idea in which we have little or no confidence, because it has little or no supporting evidence, is frequently called a *hypothesis*. An idea in which scientists have a great deal of confidence, because it is well confirmed by evidence, is frequently called a *theory*. The word *law* is used to mean an idea that has been universally accepted on the basis of an overwhelming amount of evidence. These linguistic conventions are not strictly adhered to. For example, the word *hypothesis* is often used to mean just any idea at all, and Newton's law of gravitation has been superseded by Einstein's theory of relativity. But the ultimate difference between a hypothesis and a law is the degree of evidence. Regardless of how much evidence exists to support an idea, scientists still regard it as tentative. Even a universally accepted scientific law is only as good as the empirical evidence for it, and if new evidence indicates that a revision or rejection of the law is in order, then so be it. The greatest certainties in science are really just very high probabilities. They are not absolute certainties dogmatically embraced.

Science Has Limits

Because science is empirical, its findings are restricted to the evidence of our five senses and their extensions (for example, microscopes and telescopes). The knowledge that science brings us can never exceed the power of the tools it uses to make observations. The discovery that Jupiter has moons orbiting it, for example, had to await the invention of the telescope. The outer limits of the universe may extend beyond the 10 billion light-years that we can see, but to know this we will need even more powerful telescopes than we have now. And a cure for cancer may not come along until we discover an entirely new form of medical technology. As technology grows, so does the power of science to gain knowledge.

Not All Issues Are Scientific

Because science is concerned strictly with what is observable and quantifiable, it leaves many important issues untouched. For example, I couldn't go to scientists and ask them to prove that life is meaningful (or meaningless), that the sight of a forest of pine trees gives me profound pleasure, that the two-week-old human embryo is (or is not) a human being, that capital punishment is right (or wrong), or that God exists (or doesn't exist). These are just not issues that science deals with.

Thus, it is a mistake to think that any question that cannot be answered through empirical investigation is unimportant to us as human beings. Science can observe and verify the electrochemical behavior of my brain when I look at that pine forest or the physical behavior that I exhibit, but it does not attempt to observe and verify the pleasure I experience when doing so. It would be excessive scientism to say, "The profound pleasure you experience is nothing but an electrochemical reaction in your brain." Such a statement not only belies the fullness of human experience, it does a disservice to science as well. Science, through careful observations, can also show that capital punishment does or does not correlate with a decrease in capital crimes, but it cannot say whether the death penalty is right or wrong. This is a philosophical, not a scientific, issue.

❏ Baloney Detection

Students of mine often ask me how they can tell when a claim is true. My answer is that there really is no quick and easy way to tell. If there were, flimflam would be much less common than it is. Generally speaking, we should be skeptical of quick and easy answers. After all, it is the desire for quick and easy answers that makes New Age ideas so attractive. Perhaps the best we can do is learn to recognize some of the telltale signs of pseudoscience: vague language, evasion of falsifiability, reliance on anecdotal evidence, a negative attitude toward skepticism, and the like. These, at least, tell us when to be skeptical. Other things to watch for are expressions like:

It's scientific.
It's been proved . . .
The experts say . . .

When the evidence is not cited or the experts named, we are merely being dazzled by magical words, and we have good reason to be skeptical. But even if scientific studies are cited and the experts are named, this does not automatically mean that the claim is true. Studies can be flawed and experts mistaken, and to discover these things may take time and effort on our part. The truth is not always easy to find, and there simply is no substitute for our own active intelligence.

Scientists are human beings subject to all the foibles that afflict all other humans. Even when we read about a discovery made by a reputable scientific establishment, we should be cautious and wait for follow-up studies (replication). Remember the media's tendency to sensationalism. Remember wishful thinking. Remember human error. Remember cheating. And remember that scientists sometimes succumb to the pressure to discover. The core of scientific truths that has emerged over time is a product of an extremely laborious, self-correcting method of empirical testing; it is not just a set of pronouncements uttered by venerable people. The reason that science deserves our respect is that it questions even its own authorities and recognizes that reputation and anecdote are no substitutes for demonstrable facts.

❑ Chapter Review Questions

1. The scientist and the pseudoscientist have different attitudes toward skepticism. How are they different? Why are they different?
2. The scientist and the pseudoscientist define the open mind differently. What is the difference?
3. What is a replication study?
4. Why are replication studies important in genuine science?
5. When is an idea testable scientifically?
6. What is the attitude of many people involved in pseudoscience toward scientific testing?
7. When is an idea said to have predictive power?

8. Does the claim that we choose our own incarnations have predictive power? Why or why not?
9. What is compatibility, and why is it important in science?
10. How do scientists and pseudoscientists differ in their attitude toward compatibility?
11. What is falsifiability, and why is it important in science?
12. How do scientists differ from pseudoscientists in their attitude toward falsifiability?
13. How does science differ from pseudoscience on the issue of vague language?
14. What does it mean to say that science is empirical?
15. Why are many experiences reported by dowsers, channelers, and psychics not counted as empirical evidence of the paranormal?
16. Give an example of how a psychic or occult experience can be entirely explained by belief combined with imagination.
17. Is it true that mainstream science does not believe in the existence of anything that cannot be seen?
18. How do scientists differ from pseudoscientists in their attitude about anecdotal evidence?
19. How reliable is our own personal experience in acquiring scientific knowledge? (For example: "I know that crystals actually heal, because that's how I got rid of my asthma.")
20. What is the Fallacy of Positive Cases?
21. What advantages does a controlled study have over anecdotal evidence?
22. What is a control group?
23. What is an experimental group?
24. What is a placebo?
25. What is a blind experiment?
26. What is a double-blind experiment?
27. How much money does the American public spend on quack medicine each year?
28. What are the four possible outcomes of any treatment, and what responses are available to the quack doctor?
29. What is the shotgun effect?
30. What is the experimenter effect?
31. What is the Clever Hans Effect?
32. How does science differ from pseudoscience in regard to its capacity for self-correction?

33. What is the difference between believing and knowing?
34. Using the method of science can bring you knowledge, but using the method of pseudoscience cannot. Why is this?
35. What is the difference between a hypothesis, a theory, and a law?
36. Which one of the items mentioned in question 35 could not be overturned by new evidence?
37. In what ways is science limited?
38. In science, when is an idea considered absolutely certain?
39. Give an example of an important issue that science does not deal with. Why is it not a scientific issue?

❑ Chapter Exercises

I.

Using what you have learned from this chapter and your own good sense, determine whether the following items reflect good scientific thinking. Suggested answers to exercises 1–5 are discussed in the back of the book.

1. Many so-called scientists reject astrology without ever having studied it. But how can they judge something that they know nothing about?
2. In order to get proof of ESP, you must first believe in it.
3. I have experienced clairvoyance twice in my life. The first time was when my mother died: I had a vision of her dying at the moment she died. The second time was when my wife went into labor: I was across town, yet I could feel her contractions. When clairvoyance happens, it's the real thing, and I can always tell when it's the real thing.
4. Some channelers say that there are 7 astral planes, and some say that there are 12. But so what! Even scientists disagree with one another. For example, many scientists are arguing about whether electromagnetic fields given off by power lines cause cancer. So, the channelers are no worse than the scientists.
5. The only valid way to tell whether something is real is to try it yourself and see whether it works for you.
6. Just after we moved in, we were told that this house was haunted. We were skeptical at first, but just to make sure, we called in Alex-

andra, a psychic, to get verification. Sure enough, Alexandra said she could sense the presence of three ghosts: a mother, father, and son.

7. The psychic Madam X said they would find the body of the little girl in the northwest corner of the junkyard. They did! Doesn't that prove that some psychics are genuine?

8. Scientists don't want to admit the reality of psychokinesis, because this would mean that they would have to throw out much of what they have been taught.

9. The National Research Council of the National Academy of Sciences looked at the best-documented cases of psychic phenomena, including mental telepathy and psychokinesis. It found that the laboratory studies of psychic phenomena were plagued by sloppy methodology and inadequate security against fraud. But proponents of psychic phenomena denounced the council as biased and dominated by skeptics (Levine, 1988).

10. Science hasn't proved that ESP exists. But so what! Science cannot even prove that love exists, and obviously love does exist. So, the fact that science hasn't proved that ESP exists doesn't mean that ESP doesn't exist.

11. One day, many years ago, I experienced mental telepathy: I knew that a perfect stranger was thinking about a sailboat seconds before he began talking about it. That experience has never happened again. But that time it was genuine telepathy.

12. I don't care if astrology is pseudoscience. It works!

13. Mary went to an acupuncturist and had a pin put in her ear in order to lose weight. In seven months she lost 75 pounds. Obviously, this method really works.

14. News report: "Evidently, a new cure for insomnia has been found. Seventeen people from the Los Angeles area reported that they had solved their problem of sleeplessness by eating popcorn just before retiring at night."

15. Science hasn't proved ESP, but then science hasn't really proved *anything* absolutely.

II.

Decide whether the following items can be tested. If so, how? If not, why not? Suggested answers to exercises 1–4 are given in the back of the book.

1. The presence of skeptical people destroys psychic phenomena (seances, telepathy, levitation, psychokinesis), because the skeptical mind produces a form of negative energy that interferes with or jams the psychic energy field.
2. The amazing Razco has the ability to see auras. The aura is the field of psychic energy that extends three feet in all directions from the body. It is, to one who can read it, a perfect indicator of a person's life and personality.
3. I know Uri Geller is a fake. I know there are lots of fakes. But I know a woman who is a genuine psychic. I mean, she predicts the future, and she can actually read another person's mind.
4. Astrologer: "You will experience an important change in your love life next year."
5. Ron Hastings is a channeler. But he's different from other channelers because he channels a living person; he channels his own brother Dave.
6. How do you know that the airline crash in Scotland wasn't caused by ghosts? They haven't found the reason yet, so it *could* have been ghosts.
7. I have a neighbor who can levitate.
8. "We have earthquakes and tornadoes because there are too many people in the world who lack self-love" [Penny Torres].
9. Many women (and a few men) have intuition.
10. Penny Torres is a channeler for a man named Mafu who lived in the first century in Pompeii.
11. Bill Tinudo is a channeler for John Lennon [New Age Expo, 1989].
12. Neville Rowe is a channeler for dolphins [New Age Expo, 1989].
13. The Amazing Doctor D has the gift of seeing spirits. Many people who have been molested by a ghost come to her. She helps them by seeing the ghost and performing an exorcism [*Sally Jessy Raphael* show, 1988].
14. If you keep a crystal on your body at all times, any injury you have will heal in half the time normally required.
15. Shirley MacLaine can leave her body and visit any of the other planets in our solar system.
16. Charles Spaegel is the reincarnation of Napoleon Bonaparte [*Stanley Tonight* show, 1985].
17. Angela Altomari can do psychometry. This means that she can hold something of yours, like a ring or a watch, and tell you important information about yourself [*Donahue* show, 1986].

APPENDIX

❏ ❏ ❏ ❏ ❏ ❏ ❏

Further Illustrations

1. *Paradox.* How superstition can be responsible for paradox is illustrated in the following example:

[The statement on this page in brackets is false.]

The statement in brackets is paradoxical, because it entails a contradiction: if it is true, it must be false, and if it is false, it must be true!

We become entangled in paradox here only because we assume that words mean something independently of their use by a person who is speaking. In doing this, we grant words a power completely detached from any human agency. (This is superstition that violates basic principle 2.) The solution to the paradox is merely to remember that words don't refer, people do. Hence, the statement in brackets is meaningless, because it is not being used by anyone to say something. The paradox is created only because we (superstitiously) regard the statement as referring to itself by itself.

2. *Contradiction and nonsense.* To say that God can perform a contradiction (for example, God can make a square circle) is to utter nonsense, because a contradiction is nonsense. If x is nonsense, so is the statement "God can make an x." Because *square circle* conveys no information, "God can make a square circle" conveys no information either.

To see this, make up a nonsense term like *mumsidith*. Now stick "God can make a . . ." in front of it. Does this help? Does the resulting sentence make sense? Obviously not, because the nonsense term makes nonsense out of the entire sentence.

145

3. *Empirical criteria.*   Imagine a 17-year-old girl saying to her 10-year-old sister: "I can't describe what it's like to fall in love, but when it happens to you, you'll know it." A few years later, the younger sister falls in love and is aware that she has done so. But how can she know that she's in love if she doesn't know what to look for? The answer is that she actually does know what to look for. Even when she was too young to fully understand romantic love, she learned how to tell when someone was in love: she observed (from the outside) what the indications were; that is, she observed the circumstances and the behavior of her lovesick sister.

If we really had no way of identifying (no criteria for) being in love, we could never know when and if it happened. The term *in love* would be empirically meaningless and could not be used to communicate empirical information.

4. *Precognition.*   What about this possibility: You attempt to falsify your own precognition (of your being in an accident on the freeway) by staying in bed all day, but you fall asleep watching soap operas, and some of your friends come over and carefully lift you into their car and take you for a ride on the freeway. Soon after, there is an accident, and your prediction comes true.

Now, if this happened, should we say that it proved precognition? No, because this is an isolated case and, as such, it is merely a curious quirk of fate. We could, if we wanted, find many such isolated anecdotes and weave them together to make it look as if precognition were a common and real phenomenon. (This is the stuff that fringe literature is made of.) But in doing this, we would be counting the hits and ignoring the misses. In other words, we would be committing the Fallacy of Selective Perception. From a scientific point of view we should not be impressed unless a person is able to make predictions that consistently come true in spite of our efforts to falsify them. This, of course, is not a test that anyone could pass.

Let's try another angle: suppose we say that a precognitive impression will come true *if no one does anything to prevent it*. The problem with this idea is that it still implies a contradiction, because it implicitly admits that something can be done to prevent it. Remember, a genuine precognition is knowing what *will* happen, and it is a contradiction to say that what will happen can be prevented.

How about this: a precognition will come true if nobody knows about it. The problem with this statement is that somebody has to know about it. The person who has the precognitive impression has to know about it, and that person is in a position to prevent it. Incidently, it shouldn't matter how many people know about it, because, by definition, the event must happen regardless.

And how about this: what if the prediction is about something that human beings have no control over, for example, a supernova? This is a curious question, because there should be no limits on the types of events that can be foretold. After all, the future contains *all* events, those that we can control as well as those that we can't.

CSICOP keeps records of psychic predictions, the misses as well as the hits. The number of misses (when the language is specific enough to make checking possible) is vastly greater than the number of hits. Are you surprised? (See *Skeptical Inquirer,* Fall 1982.)

5. *Proving a negative.* Actually, we can and do frequently prove negatives. For example: "Harold has no [dental] cavities." By careful inspection of Harold's mouth, we could verify and prove that this negative statement is true. Why is this? Because two conditions are met: (1) the item in question (a dental cavity) is a descriptive concept, and (2) a limited domain is specified (Harold's mouth) in which to search. In other words, the negative proposition is provable because it talks about something that we can recognize when we see it and because it specifies where we are to do the looking. If either one of these conditions is missing, a negative proposition cannot be proved. For example, "Dental cavities do not exist" could not be proved true even if it were true. Even though we have a descriptive concept, this negative statement could never be proved, because no definite domain is specified. Even if we checked every person in the world and none of them had any cavities, it would not prove this negative proposition, because it would always be possible that cavities existed somewhere else.

"There are no ghosts in Harold's bedroom" could not be proved, even though we have a specific domain, because the concept of a ghost is not descriptive in a way that would enable us to reliably identify something as a ghost. Of course, there are sightings that make some people say that they saw a ghost, but this is only their personal interpretation of what they saw. Nonbelievers would have a different interpretation even if they saw the same things that the believers saw. (Notice that this is not the case with cavities. Even nonbelievers would be converted by what they saw if they were shown a few good specimens.)

6. *"Nothing is certain."* If we analyze further the claim that nothing is certain, we will discover that it is actually incoherent. In order for the term *uncertain* to be meaningful, the term *certain* must also be meaningful, because the former is just the negation of the latter. (Consider

adequate-inadequate, active-inactive, audible-inaudible, and so on.) In other words, the expression *being uncertain* can be sensibly applied only if the expression *being certain* can. If we can imagine no case that is certain, it is meaningless to call anything *un*certain. The term *uncertain* loses its meaning.

The reason that it is meaningful (in everyday conversation) to say that something is uncertain is that we acknowledge that certainty is possible. In other words, when we say that something is uncertain, we are implying some procedure that would have provided certainty. For example, Joe was not certain that the president had come to the party because he had not attended the party. But Joe could have been certain if he had been there.

So, returning to an intelligible sense of the word *certain,* we can be certain that people have clairvoyance, for example, if they really have it. A simple test can be designed that would verify it beyond any reasonable doubt. Thus, "We can be certain of nothing" cannot serve as an excuse when a psychic is tested for ESP and fails to demonstrate it.

7. *"The mind is a mysterious entity."* We may not know all there is to know about the mind, but this is no reason to think that the mind has boundless potential, still less that it is a mysterious entity. In fact, there is really no good reason to think that what we call our mind is any sort of entity at all. That we do have a mind is beyond question. That is to say, we think, dream, experience, calculate, judge, imagine, and so on. But the idea that we possess a thing (an entity) called the mind in the same way that we possess a brain is a popular (very popular) myth.

The feeling of mystery about the mind has undoubtedly been generated by regarding the mind as a thing, for as a thing, it must be a very special sort of thing because it has no color, shape, or size and occupies no space. How we came to regard the mind as an entity is probably explained by the factors of language, culture, and religion.

8. *Out-of-body experiment.* How could we test people (even ourselves) in order to verify a real OBE? One suggestion is to have them retrieve some information about a faraway location that is unknown to them. This would indeed prove something (if it happened). There have been experiments of this kind, but none of them has produced convincing evidence. There is an interesting complication here: if such an experiment were successful, it would not necessarily mean that an out-of-body experience had occurred, because the same result could be explained as clairvoyance or mental telepathy.

ANSWERS TO EXERCISES

Answers for Chapter 1
Language: The Starting Point

1. Verbal disagreement. "Educated." Mary: having a degree; getting professional experience. Ellen: knowing a broad range of subjects.
2. Factual disagreement. This issue can be settled by making *in utero* observations of the developing embryo.
3. Verbal disagreement. "Intelligent." Trish: can be trained to do tricks and respond to verbal orders. Tony: can do reading, writing, and arithmetic.
4. Verbal disagreement. "Natural." Trudy: practiced by all (or nearly all) people. Mabel: practiced by other kinds of animals.
5. Factual disagreement. This issue can be settled by scientific investigation.
6. Verbal disagreement. "Sound." Stan: a sensation experienced by a living creature. Millie: a vibration of the air.
7. Verbal disagreement. "Religion." Nate: a set of beliefs about reality and living. Connie: a belief in God or a set of beliefs centering on God.
8. Factual disagreement. Historical research can settle this question: church records, family diaries, and the like.
9. Verbal disagreement. "Obscene." Kate: showing explicit sexual acts. Mort: showing violence.
10. Verbal disagreement. "Democracy." Steve: The people, directly or

indirectly, govern themselves. Bruno: The people directly govern themselves.

11. Verbal disagreement. "Living things." Scientist 1: have DNA; use other cells to make copies of themselves. Scientist 2: can reproduce themselves; can manufacture proteins.

12. Factual disagreement. Settle this one by investigating museums containing Hitler's remains; witnesses' reports; rumors of his whereabouts in South America, and so forth.

13. Verbal disagreement. "Dead." Drake: no heartbeat, no respiration. Glenda: no brainwaves.

14. Verbal disagreement. "Christian." Henry: belief in peace and justice through passive resistance. Conrad: belief that Jesus was the only true son of God.

❑ Answers for Chapter 2
What Are We Saying?

I.

A. (Fairly Easy)

1. Empirical statement. We know what experiences we'll have if it's true, and we know what experiences we'll have if it's false. If the statement is true and if we search carefully and thoroughly enough, we will encounter a hairy creature resembling a human in its erect posture but standing 8 to 10 feet tall and weighing 500 to 800 pounds. If the statement is false, we will not encounter this creature.

2. Attitude statement. The person is primarily expressing feelings about apartheid.

3. Analytic statement. We ordinarily use the word *hat* to mean something worn on the head. The statement, therefore, is true by definition.

4. Empirical statement. This speaker is describing the experiences that we will have if we go to Africa and count the elephants.

5. Metaphysical statement. The term *heaven* is (probably) being used to refer to a supernatural realm. Hence, the statement does not describe any sense experiences that we can have.

B. *(Moderately Difficult)*

21. Attitude statement. The speaker is not describing a fact that we can observe, because people are not literally born equal in any respect. The statement is expressing feelings about people and perhaps commanding us to give equal treatment to all people.
22. Analytic statement. If the speaker means that God existed before He existed in order to bring Himself into existence, this statement is a contradiction (paradox).
23. Value statement. This statement contains a value term. Thus it qualifies as a value judgment if the speaker can provide descriptive criteria for *wrong* and allows falsifiability. If the speaker would allow no conceivable facts to falsify the statement, then he or she is merely expressing an attitude.

II.

1. This statement is empirically meaningful, because the term *unicorn* is a descriptive one. Thus, we know what we will experience if the statement is false, and we know what we will not experience if it's true.
2. This speaker would probably point out some things that, she believes, verify her statement—for example, that computers solve math problems. On the other hand, she could probably conceive of nothing that would make her change her mind. Hence, because her statement is not falsifiable, it has no empirical meaning.
3. The speaker would most likely point to confirming instances but would allow nothing to count against his claim. If one gets what one prays for, this "proves" it, but if one does not get what one prays for, this does not falsify it. Hence, the statement has no empirical meaning. It merely expresses an attitude.

III.

1. Analytic statement. The speaker is defining any human action as "doing it for yourself." The statement "Every act is selfish," therefore, is true by definition and could not be falsified (or verified) by sense experience. It also expresses an attitude: it shows us how the speaker feels about human beings.

2. Value statement. The statement is empirically significant: we can observe people getting excited (or not) by the occult. But it is a bit vague: how many people have to get excited in order for the statement to be counted true?

3. Attitude statement. MacLaine is undoubtedly thinking of the law of conservation of matter and energy. This scientific law does not, however, say that living creatures don't die. MacLaine would most likely allow no conceivable observations to falsify her claim. Thus, she is merely expressing her feelings about death.

❑ Answers for Chapter 3
Common Fallacies

I. Arguments

1. Premise: Jake hangs around with communists.

   Conclusion: Therefore, Jake is a communist.

2. Premise: The butler was not at the house at the time (of the murder).

   Conclusion: Therefore, the butler could not have killed the maid.

3. No argument.

4. Premises: 1. Arch supports reduce pain.
                 2. Arch supports improve your disposition.

   Conclusion: Therefore, arch supports can actually lengthen your life.

5. No argument.

6. Premises: 1. More and more babies are born every year.
                 2. Every year there is less and less food to feed the babies who are born.

   Conclusion: Therefore, there is sure to be a crisis in the near future.

7. Premises: 1. If there is life on Jupiter, there is available oxygen there.

2. There is no available oxygen on Jupiter.

Conclusion: Therefore, there is no life on Jupiter.

8. Premises: 1. All linguists speak at least two languages.
2. Harvey is a linguist.

Conclusion: Therefore, Harvey speaks at least two languages.

9. Premises: 1. There's much evidence that UFOs are real.
2. The newspaper said that last year over 300 UFO sightings were reported.

Conclusion: Therefore, at least some UFOs are real.

10. Premises: 1. Either they'll find a cure for AIDS, or there will be an epidemic.
2. They will not find a cure for AIDS.

Conclusion: Therefore, there's sure to be an epidemic.

11. Premise: All the newspapers say that Collier won the election.

Conclusion: Therefore, Collier is the new president.

12. Premises: 1. If Tom had ESP, he would have known that his wife was being unfaithful.
2. Tom did not know that his wife was being unfaithful.

Conclusion: Therefore, Tom doesn't have ESP.

13. No argument.

14. Premise: All newspapers distort facts to sell stories.

Conclusion: Therefore, you can never trust the newspapers.

15. Premises: 1. Lizzy Borden was the only one else at home at the time that her parents were murdered.
2. The neighbors saw no one going to or coming from the house at the time of the murder.

Conclusion: Therefore, Lizzy Borden committed the murder.

16. Premises: 1. If everyone were honest, we wouldn't need to put locks on our doors.

2. Not everyone is honest.
_____

Conclusion: Therefore, we have to put locks on our doors.

17. Unclear. The person may be making the following argument:
    Premises: 1. Abortion is murdering an innocent person.
                   2. Abortion is a crime against humanity.
_____

Conclusion: Anyone who favors abortion is an enemy of the human race.

It's possible that the person is not making an argument at all.

II. Common Fallacies

1. Two Wrongs 2. Bandwagon 3. Irrelevant Thesis 4. Begging the Question 5. Appeal to Authority 6. Equivocation ("connected") 7. False Cause 8. Appeal to Ignorance 9. ad Hominem 10. Bandwagon 11. Loaded Question 12. False Dichotomy 13. Poisoning the Well 14. Past Practice 15. Hasty Generalization 16. Genetic 17. Bandwagon 18. Equivocation ("spirit") 19. Appeal to Ignorance 20. False Cause 21. Genetic 22. Straw Man 23. False Cause 24. Begging the Question 25. Appeal to Authority 26. Hasty Generalization 27. Irrelevant Thesis 28. Begging the Question 29. Genetic 30. False Cause 31. Poisoning the Well 32. False Dichotomy 33. Straw Man 34. ad Hominem 35. Two Wrongs 36. Past Practice 37. Loaded Question

❑ Answers for Chapter 4
The Paranormal

1. This statement shows ignorance of the fact that extensive scientific attempts have been made to validate psychic phenomena and other paranormal events.
2. This statement is simply not true. The main purpose of science is to find the explanation for things that are not understood.
3. This is strange reasoning. It is very easy to understand how the myth continues: many people are eager to believe; the media pander to this eagerness by telling exciting stories and failing to tell the disappointing facts behind them; myth making is profitable; and so on. What is not so easy to understand is why, if his power is real,

Geller can't convince the skeptics and why he refuses to be tested by magicians.

4. This claim provides charlatans with a handy excuse whenever their power fails. But even if we allow this excuse, we can still test and validate a paranormal power, if it is real.

5. If this were true, we should expect an abundance of scientific evidence for psychic power. But in fact, there isn't even a scrap of it. Many people think that they have evidence of ESP, but careful examination shows that they enjoy an illusion created by uncritical thinking.

6. The harm is that many people need, and can benefit from, genuine medical treatment. For these people a delay could be serious, even fatal.

7. Not quite. Logical impossibilities are not possible, and we shouldn't even waste our time trying to get evidence for them. It would be futile to try to prove an incoherent, nonsensical idea. Examples: precognition and time travel.

8. How could we know that levitation is *not* real? This we cannot do, because we cannot prove a negative. The statement also suggests that a lack of proof that levitation does not exist is reason to believe that it does. This is the fallacy of appealing to ignorance.

9. All forms of psychotherapy work to some degree (see Hilgard, 1979), and the particular method has little to do with the obtained results. Successful psychotherapy depends more on the caring, concerned atmosphere in which it is conducted than on the theory and method employed by the therapist.

10. This is the fallacy of explaining a coincidence, and, hence, needs no explanation. Also, this person could easily be imagining more detailed correspondence between his impression and the later event than was actually there. There is no way to check the event (the broken ankle) against the mental picture he had six months before.

❏ Answers for Chapter 5
Science versus Pseudoscience

I.

1. We do not need to know *how* something works in order to test it and verify *that* it works. Numerous tests of astrology have been

done, and they show that it does not work. (See *Skeptical Inquirer,* Spring, 1986.)

2. This is just what we would expect if psychic experience is largely the work of the imagination. But even if it's true that one must first believe in it, it can still be tested. All we need to do is use believers as subjects. On the other hand, if the speaker means that the experimenters must be believers, this takes the matter outside of science, because nothing is considered proved in science until it satisfies the skeptics.

3. These are interesting anecdotes, but in order to get scientific proof of this type of thing, we need to see repeatable results. If the clairvoyant intuitions come on at odd times, we can still keep records and check them out, being careful to count the misses as well as the hits. The casual observing that this person has done is simply not good enough to warrant his conclusion.

4. When scientists disagree over scientific issues, the dispute can be resolved in time by the growth of scientific knowledge. The jury is still out on the question of electromagnetic fields causing cancer, but the answer will probably be found within a few years. But when two persons disagree over how many astral planes exist, scientific resolution is impossible, because astral planes are not supposed to be accessible to the five senses.

5. The person who made this statement is simply unaware of how easy it is to be mistaken. Scientists require controlled studies precisely because the "personal-experience" approach is so unreliable. The pervasiveness of this kind of thinking makes fraud and charlatanism very profitable.

II.

1. This assertion overlooks the numerous cases in which psychic phenomena have reportedly taken place in the presence of skeptical people. But even if we grant that the assertion is true, a test can easily be arranged in which all skeptics are removed from the test area and the experiment is observed by video cameras. In other words, it is still possible to obtain proof of psychic phenomena, if they do exist.

2. This is a testable idea. Simply have Razco look at an open doorway and tell whether the person on the other side standing next to the doorway (but out of sight) is on the right or the left. People who

think they can see auras most likely are combining a strong belief with a rich imagination.

3. If this woman can really read another person's mind, her ability can be verified quite easily: Go to her and ask her what you are thinking. And if she can really tell, it can be demonstrated for all the world to see, using the Zener cards. But considering the negative results of past experiments with mental telepathy, the woman probably has no such power. Predicting the future is logically impossible, because it's an incoherent idea (see Chapter 4). Her predictions that happen to come true must be weighed against those that don't. Some are bound to come true because of the shotgun effect.

4. This statement of the astrologer is too vague to be tested scientifically. What kind of a change? Is it for the better or for the worse? Important in what way?

REFERENCES

❑ ❑ ❑ ❑ ❑ ❑ ❑

Abell, G. O., and Singer, B. *Science and the Paranormal*. New York: Charles Scribner's, 1981.

"And a Child Shall Lead Them—Astray." *Discover,* May 1984.

Bartholomew, R. E. "The Airship Hysteria of 1896–97." *Skeptical Inquirer,* Winter 1990.

Berlitz, Charles. *The Bermuda Triangle*. New York: Avon Books, 1978.

Bernstein, Ellen. "Lourdes," in *Medical and Health Annual*. Chicago: Encyclopedia Britannica, 1982.

Cazeau, C. J. "Prophecy: The Search for Certainty." *Skeptical Inquirer,* Fall 1982.

Cheetham, Erika. *The Man Who Saw Tomorrow*. New York: Berkeley Books, 1973.

Coon, Dennis. *Introduction to Psychology,* 4th ed. St. Paul, Minn.: West Publishing, 1986.

Diaconis, Persi. "Statistical Problems in ESP Research," in *A Skeptic's Handbook of Parapsychology,* Paul Kurtz, ed. Buffalo: Prometheus Books, 1985.

Discover. P.O. Box 420087, Palm Coast, FL 32142-0087.

Frazier, K. "Lonely UFO Vigil Ends in Death for Woman." *Skeptical Inquirer,* Spring 1983.

Gardner, Martin. *Fads and Fallacies in the Name of Science*. New York: Dover Publications, 1957.

Hansel, C. E. M. "The Search for a Demonstration of ESP," in *A Skeptic's Handbook of Parapsychology,* Paul Kurtz, ed. Buffalo: Prometheus Books, 1985.

Harris, Melvin. "Are Past-Regressions Evidence for Reincarnation?" *Free Inquiry,* Fall 1986.

Hilgard, Ernest. *Introduction to Psychology,* 7th ed. New York: Harcourt Brace Jovanovich, 1979.

———. "Hypnosis Gives Rise to Fantasy and Is Not a Truth Serum." *Skeptical Inquirer,* Spring 1981.

Hoebens, P. H. "The Modern Revival of Nostradamitis." *Skeptical Inquirer,* Fall 1982.

Hume, David. *Enquiries Concerning Human Understanding and Concerning the Principles of Morals.* Oxford: Clarendon Press, 1975. Originally published 1777.

Kane, Margaret Fox. "Spiritualism Exposed: Margaret Fox Kane Confesses to Fraud," in *A Skeptic's Handbook of Parapsychology,* Paul Kurtz, ed. Buffalo: Prometheus Books, 1985.

Klass, Philip. *UFOs: The Public Deceived.* Buffalo: Prometheus Books, 1983.

———. *UFO Abductions: A Dangerous Game.* Buffalo: Prometheus Books, 1988.

Kurtz, Paul. *The Transcendental Temptation.* Buffalo: Prometheus Books, 1986.

———. "A Case Study of the West Pittston 'Haunted' House." *Skeptical Inquirer,* Winter 1986–1987.

Kusche, Lawrence. *The Bermuda Triangle Mystery—Solved.* New York: Warner Books, 1975.

The Laser. Newsletter of the Southern California Skeptics, Los Angeles.

Levine, A. "The Twilight Zone in Washington." *U.S. News & World Report,* December 5, 1988.

MacLaine, Shirley. *Out on a Limb.* New York: Bantam Books, 1983.

Marshall, Charles. *Vitamins and Minerals: Help or Harm?* Philadelphia: George F. Stickey, 1986.

NCAHF Newsletter. National Council against Health Fraud, Box 1276, Loma Linda, CA 92354.

Randi, James. *The Truth about Uri Geller.* Buffalo: Prometheus Books, 1975.

———. *Flim-Flam!* Buffalo: Prometheus Books, 1982.

———. "Allison and the Atlanta Murders: A Follow-Up." *Skeptical Inquirer,* Winter 1982–1983.

———. "The Project Alpha Experiment Part 2: Beyond the Laboratory." *Skeptical Inquirer,* Fall 1983.

Sabom, M. B. *Recollections of Death: A Medical Investigation.* New York: Simon & Schuster, 1982.

Sagan, Carl. *Cosmos*. New York: Random House, 1980.

Sanduleak, N. "The Moon Is Acquitted of Murder in Cleveland." *Skeptical Inquirer,* Spring 1985.

The Skeptical Inquirer. Box 229, Buffalo, NY 14215-0229.

Steiner, R. "Live TV Special Explores, Tests Psychic Powers." *Skeptical Inquirer,* Fall 1989.

Terrace, H. "The Nim Chimsky Controversy," in *Introductory Psychology,* by Daniel Goleman et al., 2nd ed. New York: Random House, 1982.

INDEX

161